The original edition of this book is dedicated to the memory of my dear parents Annie and Charles Allchild, to Norah James for her inspiring inscription and to Fitzrovians throughout the world.

I dedicate this new edition to the memory of my late husband Arthur. His love, patience, belief and encouragement in everything I have achieved gave me the inspiration to carry on.

Sally Fiber was born in the Fitzroy Tavern in 1936, the only child of Annie and Charles Allchild, and lived there until her late teens. After attending St George's School, Harpenden, she qualified as a beauty specialist. In 1960 she founded the Northwood group of the League of Jewish Women and, despite contracting MS in the 1970s, Sally has maintained a full lecture programme and increased her involvement in voluntary work. In 1983 she was made a Life Member of the National Council of the League in recognition of her work.

In 1990, Sally established and spearheaded the 'Jewish West End Project', which in turn mounted a major exhibition – *Living Up West: Jewish Life in London's West End* – and published a book of the same name. Married with two children and six grandchildren, she lives in Northwood, Middlesex.

Clive Powell-Williams is the author of several works, including *With All Thy Might* and *Cold Burial.* He gained a law degree at University College, London, and an English and History degree from the Open University. He was head of history at St Martin's preparatory school, Northwood, where he taught for twenty years. He is married to a fellow teacher and has two children and six grandchild,

To Orlandos William
Best Wishes
Sally Fiber
12 August 2015

The Fitzroy

The Autobiography of a London Tavern

Sally Fiber's story of The Fitzroy
as told to
Clive Powell-Williams

Published by Sally Fiber
in conjunction with DeSapinaud

ISBN: 978-0-9928850-0-7

Printed and bound in Great Britain by:
Book Printing UK, Remus House, Coltsfoot Drive,
Woodston, Peterborough PE2 9BF

Fitzrovia was the name given to Bohemian London in the first half of this century as a result of writers, artists and politicians frequenting the Fitzroy Tavern. Born and brought up in the Fitzroy during its heyday, Sally Fiber draws on her own memories as well as family archives, to recall the special place, time and state of mind that was Fitzrovia. As the child and grandchild of the Tavern's licensees, she provides a unique record of the years when, for example, Augustus John drew a self-portrait in her mother's autograph book, and when Wynford Vaughan-Thomas held a memorial service in the bar for Dylan Thomas. Then, during the Second World War, the Tavern adopted a minesweeper called HMS *Fitzroy* and the collection of wartime memorabilia multiplied and became a feature of the tavern. A most unusual charity was established, as habitués would aim paper darts containing money at the ceiling – then, once a year, these 'Pennies From Heaven' would be taken down by a celebrity and used to fund outings and later, parties for deprived children.

But whilst the sense of the rich and the famous shines through, so too does a more shadowy world. For the Tavern was also the haunt of detectives Bob Fabian and Jack Capstick, the Public Executioner Albert Pierrepoint and politicians Hugh Gaitskell and Tom Driberg. Murder, intrigue and even a police raid on the Fitzroy – which culminated in a fierce courtroom battle – reveal the other side of this London pub.

Full of incident and anecdote, *The Fitzroy* ensures that the days of laughter, triumph and tragedy come to life once more.

'If you haven't visited the Fitzroy, you haven't visited London.' –
Augustus John

Self-portrait of Augustus John drawn in the Fitzroy

CONTENTS

FOREWORD

My first introduction to Fitzrovia's headquarters, the Fitzroy Tavern, was when I was at Cambridge in, I think, 1931-32. My introducer was Wynyard Browne, the author of *The Holly and the Ivy*, and a great friend at Cambridge. I remember well Pop Kleinfeld, who had originally been a tailor at Wall's of Eton, my Eton tailors, and we struck up a friendship discussing olden days and how tailoring had disimproved.

In 1935 I became a regular at the Fitzroy when I first went to Fleet Street as a reporter, calling in for a pint on the way home from work, unless I was on a late shift. I met many friends there, some of whom remained friends until they died. Among them were Betty May, Nina Hamnett and Sylvia Gough. Sylvia was a girlfriend of Fred Brockway's who had been to the same pension as myself in Paris. Betty May was named Tiger Woman and lived up to her reputation. Nina was a lasting friend. I saw her in Galway, where she stayed with Michael Shaw Taylor. She gave us a beautiful drawing of hers as a wedding present. After my wife left the Foreign Office she worked at John Lewis just round the corner and we used to meet regularly on Saturday mornings in the Fitzroy.

One of the occasions I remember best was Sally's father and mother's wedding, which seemed to last for days. Other acquaintances were Pierrepoint, the last hangman who told me he had a good business in Ireland as he did not have to provide a new rope for each hanging, which was not the case in England. Another was Fabian of the Yard, who was also a regular at the Fitzroy Tavern.

As one of the oldest Fitzrovians, I am delighted Sally is writing this book. Her mother was certainly 'The Mother of Fitzrovia' although her grandfather was originally the landlord. The whole place took on a new lease of life and my wife and I were honoured to be Presidents of the annual outing and Christmas party which arose from the money collected on the ceiling, as recorded in the book.

Fitzrovia replaced Bloomsbury across the other side of the Tottenham Court Road and pre-dated Soho, to which we went because the drinking hours were half an hour later. That was the only reason we ever crossed Oxford Street.

Lord Killanin

PREFACE

Augustus John aptly described the Fitzroy as 'the Clapham Junction of the world'. In its heyday this London tavern was the most loved, frequented and renowned in the world. For forty years it attracted the imagination of many, and its famous and infamous, colourful, motley clientele have been the subject of many books and television and radio programmes. Yet it was not just the customers with their compelling stories that make this such an intriguing saga, but the whole atmosphere created first by the Kleinfelds and then the Allchilds. Their warmth and generosity generated a special Fitzroy spirit and, with the innovations they introduced, made the Tavern into something unique.

Over the years, the Kleinfeld and Allchild families collected a treasure trove of material, which many writers have used in books and publications. In particular Denise Hooker, in her biography *Nina Hamnett, Queen of bohemia*, sought much information on her subject from my parents, which she readily acknowledged. Similarly Hugh David's *The Fitzrovians* and Daniel Farson's *Soho in the Fifties* made references and paid tribute to Pop Kleinfeld and the Allchilds, as did Augustus John, Albert Pierrepoint, Ralph Reader, Bob Fabian, Karl Gullers, Michael Parkin, Tom Driberg, Leslie Hunter, Judith Summers, Ian Mackay, Wynford Vaughan-Thomas and Beverley Nichols. My appreciation goes to all the authors who have let me use extracts from their books or have added their own recollections to the story.

More recently, in June 1990, The Jewish West End Project was launched, co-ordinated by me under the auspices of The London Museum of Jewish Life. The enterprise culminated in a major exhibition portraying the vibrant Jewish community that settled in London's West End, with the companion book, *Living Up West*, which mentions the early years of the Kleinfeld family and indeed the Fitzroy. I am most indebted to the curator Rickie Burman and author Gerry Black and everyone connected with the Project.

This brings me to my personal involvement in this autobiography. I was born in the Fitzroy and for the first twenty years of my life it was my home, apart from periods during the war and when I was at boarding school. So I met many of the famous customers with whom Charlie and Annie had become friends and confidants. But it was only long after my parents' retirement from the Fitzroy that I became aware of the need for a permanent record. It was a chance remark by them in 1981, 'Did you realise we would be celebrating twenty-five years of retirement from the Fitzroy?' that sparked off an indomitable personal interest in their story. I started to give talks on the subject to numerous groups. The interest increased as each talk brought me in touch with former Fitzrovians who supplemented and verified the tale. Annie and Charlie too over the next years recalled many anecdotes which might otherwise have been lost for ever. One day whilst delving through some of the incredible mass of documents, photos and other personal items of my parents, I discovered a book dedicated to me, Sally Thelma Allchild, by the celebrated novelist of the thirties Norah C. James, called *The House by the Tree*. She had signed the copy, *To Sally hoping that one day she will herself write a much better book and dedicate it to me!* This had to be an omen for me to take up the gauntlet and write the Fitzroy autobiography.

The venture had been considered before. Originally James Norbury and Norah James had planned to write the text with Nina Hamnett doing line drawings for the book in the fifties, but they got no further than a synopsis. Others were later approached to take up the challenge such as Daniel Farson, Stanley Jackson and Sue Blundell, but the concept never really developed. Still I was not daunted and continued with my researches with my cousin Judi Herman and son Jon helping me. It was in fact Jon who introduced me to his former teacher and local author Clive Powell-Williams and this gave me the biggest boost that I could have received. Clive's friendship, patience, expert collation of the text, and belief as an outsider that this was a story of great work surely makes him an honorary Fitzrovian of the highest calibre!

Throughout my labours I have been encouraged by the overwhelming support of former Fitzrovians, friends and family. I would particularly like to thank Lord Killanin for the great interest he has shown in my endeavours and for writing the Foreword to this book. Above all, my dear husband Arthur's support and practical advice has been invaluable. In conclusion the publication of *The Fitzroy* fulfils the ambitions and dreams of my parents Annie and Charles Allchild, to who this book is dedicated, and the many Fitzrovians who all recognised that the story of the Fitzroy had to be told!

SALLY FIBER

1

Opening Time

It was 9 p.m. on VE night and both the public and saloon bars of the Fitzroy were jammed full of rejoicing Londoners. Servicemen and civilians hugged wives and girlfriends, linked arms and sang *Roll out the Barrel* and *Tipperary* while 'Maestro' Reg thumped out the accompaniment on the dilapidated piano. Businessmen, journalists, politicians, detectives, sportsmen, the rich, the poor, the famous and not so famous all jostled together in the delirious celebration of victory. It was an excited, hysterical hubbub as champagne corks popped and beer flowed in this temple of conviviality and shrine of Dionysus, the Fitzroy Tavern. Banknotes of all denominations festooned the ceiling as the happy customers shot their multicoloured darts of money to swell the funds. Many added to the collection of wartime memorabilia of framed Great War recruiting posters, sailors' cap tallies, regimental badges and flashes, helmets, flags, cigarette-cards, foreign stamps and other mementos.

Everybody knew the Fitzroy Tavern at the corner of Charlotte Street and Windmill Street, the famous haunt of artists and writers. The flamboyant, bearded portrait painter Augustus John could be seen knocking back double rum and brandies with the witty birdlike Queen of Bohemia, Nina Hamnett. Dylan Thomas, the Welsh poet and writer, would declaim volubly but with increasing incoherence to the eager young war correspondent Wynford Vaughan-Thomas, his compatriot and friend, before collapsing into his pint. Over the din Ralph Reader was directing the singing with gusto. These were after all the Fitzrovians, the élite of London. And presiding over this festival of fun was 'The Guv', Charlie, in his shirtsleeves, pulling foaming pints with his wife Annie in the other bar.

Many hours later, after Charles and Annie had finished drying the glasses, clearing up the debris of paper hats, streamers and confetti and generally putting the place aright, they put their arms around each other. They watched the remaining revellers cavorting outside and singing the night away, and Charlie gave her a huge hug. 'We've done well, Annie,' he said. So they had! The Fitzroy was the toast of London and dubbed the 'Rendezvous of the World'. Visitors from all parts of the globe would seek it out as soon as they came to the capital. Tom Driberg (alias William Hickey of the *Daily Express*) had given its name to the surrounding district, Fitzrovia. Annie thought how different it had all been twenty-six years before.

Annie's father, Judah Morris Kleinfeld, had sailed from Polish Russia to St Catherine's Dock, London, with his young wife Jane clutching their three-month-old baby son. With only four pennies in his pocket, Judah and his family were among a throng of excited Yiddish-speaking immigrants arriving in London to seek fame and fortune, having fled from years of pogroms and oppression in their native country. Judah was more fortunate than most as one of his elder brothers, Oisia, had left before him and was already established. Thirty-three years later, in March 1919, Judah became the proud landlord of the newly named Fitzroy Tavern.

In the intervening years the Kleinfelds had had two more sons, Charlie and Dave, and in 1904 Jane gave birth to her only daughter, a very small baby weighing three or four pounds, whom they named Annie. The family lived at 4 Phoenix Street, just off Charing Cross Road. It was also in 1904 that Judah decided to become a British subject, an important action for his future life. Judah had started work in tailoring, the profession his father passed on to all his sons, first as a presser and later as a master tailor in Savile Row. Such was his personality and charm that he was often asked to measure as well as make the clothes for the famous and important customers. Annie never forgot the time when her father, after making a particularly magnificent coat for the future King of the Belgians in Crombie with an astrakhan collar, was able to make another equally fine one for himself with the left-over material.

Judah was respected by all who came to know him and he became a leading figure in the burgeoning Jewish West End community. He was a founder of the small West End Synagogue the Talmud Torah in Manette Street, and in 1903 he established a Jewish friendly society called the West London Hebrew and Divisional Society. He remained President of this society for the next fifteen years, instigating much help for the many Polish immigrants who were still arriving in this part of London.

Annie had a very happy childhood and proved to be a clever child. She won the Evelina de Rothschild Prize worth five pounds at the Westminster Jews Free School and later gained a scholarship to Burlington College. Annie hoped to go on afterwards to a finishing-school but her dreams were rudely shattered when her father asked her if she would help him run a pub. Judah had decided the time had come for him to take a huge career step and become the licensee of a public house, as in his native Poland innkeeping was often looked on as a second career. During the First World War Judah went into business with another tailor who also lived in Phoenix Street, called Feldman. They made greatcoats for the army. Part of his job was distribution and on his frequent walks along Tottenham Court Road he would wander into the rather deserted Windmill Street. On the corner stood a run-down establishment called the Hundred Marks, so named as there were many German immigrants in the area.

Judah Kleinfeld now bombarded the brewery Hoare & Co. with letters to persuade them that he was the ideal licensee. At first they thought his name Kleinfeld portrayed him as a German but eventually he was interviewed. He convinced the brewers that he was indeed a proud Polish Jew, now British subject, with tremendous personality and determination to make a success of this Tavern. Feldman had wanted to joint the venture too but was not eligible to hold a licence. Judah's foresight had paid off because he had naturalised. He impressed the brewery so much that they even gave him special permission for his under-age daughter to assist him, as his sons were all serving in the Forces. Judah was ecstatic, but not so poor Annie, whose cherished ambitions were shattered. Only out of loyalty and love for her father did she reluctantly agree. The pub was now renamed the Fitzroy Tavern.

So it was on that March morning in an almost deserted and desolate street with the snow falling, Annie paused and leant on the handle of her large broom. She was dejected and shivering with cold. Her father, a fine well-built man in an open shirt despite the cold, energetically brushed away the snow from the main doors of the huge red-bricked building and yelled out, 'Hurry up, Annie, or we won't be ready for our first customers!'

'First customers!' sighed Annie. She had so wanted to be a fine lady and here she was, working in a vulgar pub, of all places. Why had she ever agreed to help her father? The snow now cleared, Annie and Judah went back into the Fitzroy, closing the double doors behind them. Annie tried to warm herself in the public bar, where she had earlier lit a coal fire. Judah stopped as he walked over the newly laid brown patterned lino in the large L-shaped saloon bar – in contrast the floor of the public bar was strewn with sawdust. He looked round, pleased with its appearance. Rectangular heavy metal tables lined the sides of the room with long wooden benches against the walls and tubular steel chairs tucked neatly under each table. Some wooden bar stools were placed around the bar counter. The only decoration on the walls were a few huge etched Victorian mirrors, and the only item of interest was a clock made out of half a beer barrel. It had apparently stopped at the eleventh hour of the eleventh day in the eleventh month of 1918, and out of superstition no one had touched it since. Judah went to the back of the bar, stoked up the fire and then peered through the 'snob windows'. These were small decorative windows that provided a screen and prevented customers in the public bar from seeing who was in the saloon bar.

'Everything all right?' he called out to Annie in the public bar.

'Yes,' she replied, brushing her foot over the sawdust to smooth it again.

Judah returned through the bar and paused at the little passage between the two bars, which also led to the cellars. 'Better have one more check', he said to himself as he slid back the door and descended the winding flight of stairs. Directly on his left were the men's urinals and WC. Judah had done his best

4

to clean them, but the cellars were still damp and musty with a pungent, beery smell. On the right was the hand-cranked lift used to carry the bottled beer and spirits to the bars. He turned into the dingy beer cellar, where all the barrels with their metal pipes were kept so that the beer could be siphoned up. Beside each barrel was a white enamel bucket for beer slops before they were poured back into the barrel. No wastage here! Beyond the cellar was another room for storing the spirits. Satisfied all was well, he retraced his steps, glancing at the last of the cellars, a long tunnel that ran quite a distance under Charlotte Street. There the crates of bottled beer and soft drinks were housed. Just above the entrance were the flaps through which the beer was delivered by the horse-drawn drays.

'Right,' he exclaimed, his tour of inspection complete. Judah bounded up the stairs to unbolt the double doors of the saloon bar which opened onto Windmill Street. He closed the inner doors to keep out the cold, entered the public bar and unbolted the door that fronted on Charlotte Street. As he took up his position as patron of this new establishment, he briefly looked up at the dartboard he had put up for customers, not realising the significance it would have in later years. He checked his watch. It was time for opening. The Fitzroy was about to receive its first customers. But who were they going to be?

2

La Bohème

But to understand fully who the first customers of the Fitzroy might be, the history of the locality must be traced. The precise geographical and cultural demarcations of the area are rooted in the past, dating back to 1086, when the Domesday Book records that the territory was divided into four manors. One was Tottenhall, named after its owner, William de Tottenhall. The manor-house of Tottenham Court was a local landmark and at weekends Londoners would walk across the fields to the Court. At the outbreak of the Civil War in 1642, the manor-house was expropriated by Parliament and sold to a Ralph Harrison for £3,318. On the Restoration of Charles II it was repossessed by the Crown and in 1667 given to the Principal Secretary of State and a member of the Cabal, Henry Bennett, Earl of Arlington, in consideration of his services to the Crown. In 1672 the Earl's only daughter Isabella, who was only five years old, was married to Henry Fitzroy, one of Charles II's many illegitimate children by Barbara Villiers, Duchess of Cleveland. Henry was not much older himself, being only nine at the time of the marriage. He was created Earl of Euston and, three years later, Duke of Grafton. So the name of Fitz-Roy came from Henry being a bastard son of the King. Henry's son, Charles Fitzroy, became the second Duke of Grafton, and on Charles' death in 1757 his eldest grandson – another Henry – became the third Duke. He inherited the Euston Estate, while his youngest brother Charles was left the Tottenham Estate, but not the freehold. By 1768 Henry had risen to Prime Minister and with his Parliamentary majority passed an Act of Parliament in March of that year which vested the freehold with all its rights and privileges in Charles Fitzroy and his heirs for ever for the comparatively small sum of £300.

The Fitzroy lands bordered those of the Duke of Bedford, the Bloomsbury landowner, and Tottenham Court Road, which belonged to the Fitzroys, became a dividing line in the eighteenth century. Tottenham Court Road was host to an annual fair which became one of London's main attractions. In 1785 Vincero Lunardi, one of the first hot-air balloonists, made a dramatic flight, taking off from the Artillery Grounds at Moorfields and twenty minutes later descending in his spectacular red and white balloon onto Tottenham Court Road, where he was mobbed by a triumphant huge crowd. However, the event and the obstruction of the highway by the stall-holders became intolerable and in 1808 the annual fair was ended. The area was developed swiftly. By the late nineteenth century Tottenham Court Road had become the centre for many craftsmen and cabinet-makers, and furniture stores like Heal's, Maples and Catesby's were established.

To the west of Tottenham Court Road in the early 1700s part of the Fitzroy land called Home Fields was developed and this became the hub and focal point of the Fitzroy empire, Fitzroy Square. Architecturally it was one of London's finest, the gracious terraced houses built by the most fashionable architects, the Adam brothers. At the same time, south of Oxford Street, Soho Square was being constructed from a tract of land known as Soho Field. It acquired its name from the hunting cry of 'soho!' The square was first called King's Square after the architect Gregory King, and its elegant Georgian mansions looked down on the beautiful laid out gardens, of which the centre-piece was Charles II's statue atop a magnificent fountain designed by Cibber. This fountain was serviced by water pumped from a windmill on the other side Oxford Street. The windmill was originally to grind the corn grown in the adjoining fields on the estate of Tottenhall but was later converted to pump water to work the fountain, supplying an early link between Fitzrovia and Soho.

The north side of Oxford Street, developed in mid-century, included Charlotte Street, probably named after George III's Queen. In 1765 the Percy Chapel was built in Charlotte Street, directly facing a small connecting track that linked it to Tottenham Court Road. The track was named Windmill Street after the windmill. A coffee house erected in 1883 on the corner of Windmill Street and Charlotte Street was appropriately named the Fitzroy Coffee House. In 1887 this was converted by one of the most prolific builders of pubs in the Victorian era, William Mortimer Brutton. The surrounding streets, mews and crescents had given names that maintained the Fitzroy connection. So Cleveland Street was named after the Duchess of Cleveland, Grafton Street after the Duchess of Grafton and Warren Street after Charles Fitzroy's wife Anne Warren. How history was to repeat itself! Thus Fitzrovia spans from Euston Road in the north, Oxford Street in the south, Great Portland Street in the west and Grafton Street in the east, clear geographical parameters, in what are now the London Boroughs of Camden and Westminster.

Within these defined boundaries Fitzrovia, since its development in the eighteenth century, has always been associated with artists, writers and musicians. A notable eighteenth century resident at 30 Charlotte Street was the singer, composer, actor and novelist Charles Dibdin. His neighbours included Foot the actor at No. 3, and at No. 8 Richard Wilson, 'the father of English landscape painting'. In fact an art gallery opened in the street in 1814, the Dulwich Gallery. But the most famous resident was undoubtedly John Constable. He lived at 76 Charlotte Street between 1821 and 1837 and finished painting *Salisbury Cathedral* and *Hampstead Heath* there. Towards the end of the century James McNeill Whistler found inspiration in Fitzrovia, while Fitzroy Square itself was the abode of George Bernard Shaw. Roger Fry set up the Omega Studios and Workshops at 33 Fitzroy Square with the help of Vanessa Bell and Duncan Grant in 1913. Bloomsbury had come to Fitzrovia! Another influential painter who lived and worked in the area was the idiosyncratic Walter Sickert, who with patriarchal beard and eccentric dress could often be seen wandering along Charlotte Street.

The area was acquiring a cosmopolitan flavour from the foreigners living there, mainly French, German and Italian, and was the nearest equivalent to the Latin Quarter in Paris. In the wake of these renowned painters, struggling artists and immigrants came looking for cheap lodgings. Studios were

8

plentiful and the narrow streets were full of pubs and restaurants where they could meet, talk, laugh, borrow money and get drunk. These then made up the first Fitzrovians, a motley but interesting collection of people. They were writers, poets, sculptors and composers as well as artists, and cultivated an unconventional bohemian style of values. They responded to the jovial personality of the landlord at the Fitzroy Tavern. A special Fitzrovian atmosphere grew – a heady Bohemian mix in contrast to the smarter, more sophisticated Bloomsbury set, the other side of Tottenham Court Road, and also distinct from the Sohoites south of Oxford Street, 'the great divide'.

The leading light of this artistic community was Nina Hamnett, 'a legend in her own lifetime', in the words of her biographer, Denise Hooker. Born in Tenby, South Wales, the daughter of an army officer, she rebelled against her upbringing and studied at the London School of Art (Brangwyn's). Her years in Montparnasse, where she was friendly with Modigliani, and the influence of Sickert and her lover Roger Fry, helped to shape her artistic career. Not surprisingly Nina found London quite dull after her ostentatious life in Paris, although she enjoyed the Café Royal. After frequenting all the pubs in the area, she decided that the Fitzroy run by the 'amiable Papa Kleinfeld' best embodied the atmosphere of the Parisian café. Nina had an enormous following whom she introduced to the Fitzroy. Sitting erect on her bar stool, she ruled supreme as 'Queen of Bohemia'.

Her only acknowledged rival for this crown was Sylvia Gough, but Sylvia was a pale shadow of her former glory. A millionaire's daughter and once a stunning beauty, she had danced with the Ziegfeld Follies in New York and had been a model for Augustus John. But by now Sylvia was almost penniless, frail and 'skeletal', in the words of Daniel Farson. Her only pastime was to sit in the bar of the Fitzroy near the fire and ask all who came within hearing in the most polite and charming way if they would buy her a drink. Her Achilles heel had been young men who had bled her dry and this was why she was in such a pathetic state. But this Edwardian lady still retained her gentility. Bruce Bernard remembers her as 'just one of the loveliest ladies ever', and any money to spare would go on a bath.

If Nina was Queen, then the great portrait painter, Augustus John, had to be the Prince of Bohemia. Also born in Tenby, he was the Bohemian artist *par excellence*. Conspicuous with bright-red beard and tousled mane of hair under a broad-brimmed hat, he would step into the Fitzroy, his gold earrings flashing and his black cloak swirling around him. Often he would be accompanied by the wealthy and witty poet and critic Tommy Earp. Augustus became great friends with 'Pop', as Judah Kleinfeld was known. Over his usual drink of a double rum and brandy he engaged in long discussions with Pop on a variety of subjects. One such topic was the legendary Jewish spirit, 'Der Dybbuk', the spirit of a dead person that returns to possess a living one. Augustus and Tommy had been to see the Jewish Vilna Players performing a love story on this theme, a weird and disturbing play which enthralled them. It had been, of course, in Yiddish and Augustus was always urging Pop to teach this language to him. In a typical letter which he set Pop on 15th July 1929 he apologised for not being able to help with an outing. He gave a contribution instead and ended the letter, *Wishing you all the best & plenty of muzzle. Mazel*, one of the Yiddish words learnt from Pop, meant luck. In his autobiography, *Finished Touches*, Augustus said of Pop, 'He had the simplicity of a child but was no fool. If I knew the Yiddish for "gentleman", I would use it to describe Mr Kleinfeld!'

Augustus' friend Tommy Earp was quite a character himself. One New Year's Eve he disported himself naked in the fountain at Trafalgar Square. He was arrested for disturbing the peace and his case came up the next morning in the magistrates' court. Tommy made a fluent speech in defence of his actions, only to be interrupted by the magistrate, who rather testily rebuked him: 'Who do you think you are, President of the Oxford University Union?'

To this Tommy quietly replied, 'Well, actually I was President of the Union,' and the whole courtroom dissolved in laughter.

What appealed to both Tommy and Augustus, and in fact everybody that came to know him, was Pop's unique blend of humanity and sense of humour. Pop would listen gravely to the fantastic stories related to him by the strange characters who lived by odd devices in half-worlds of their own contrivance. But he had the uncanny faculty of sorting out the deserving wheat from the decorative chaff. These were men struggling to paint in back rooms or poets whose intentions were good but whose pockets were empty. Sometimes they would find that their rent had been paid 'by a friend'. Judah Kleinfeld rarely admitted these acts of benevolence and only in later years did the truth emerge. He never forgot the time when he first came to England with just fourpence in his pocket, and took pity on many of his customers who were down on their luck.

But whether they were poor or rich, he always impressed them with his impeccable dress. A gold chain hung from his waistcoat pocket and he had a perfectly groomed imperial beard and magnificent waxed moustache as befitted a former member of the Tsar's Guard. His face was always freshly barbered – he used to attend Alf Fegan's shop in Windmill Street twice a day on his way to and from the Midland Bank in Tottenham Court Road. Each morning Morrie or Alf would give him hot towels, massage, hair friction, trim and shave when needed, and see to his moustache and beard, and then carry out almost the same process every evening.

Pop was well known in the local community, which boasted many restaurants. Two local Italian restaurateurs who became particularly good friends were Desio Vaiani, who had an excellent up-market place called Vaiani's, and David Bertorelli, whose restaurant was just across the road from the Fitzroy. It first opened in 1912 but had no drinks licence, so the doors of the public bar of the Fitzroy would regularly swing open and the pretty Italian waitresses from Bertorelli's would rush in, trays in hand, to get their orders for drinks and liqueurs, much to the appreciation of the Fitzroy customers. David used to brag to Judah, 'You and I made Charlotte Street.'

Another fine restaurant in Charlotte Street was L'Etoile, a French establishment founded in 1904 at No. 30 by the Rossi family. Equally high-class was the Tour Eiffel, which was also a small hotel, run by Rudolf Stulik, a portly Viennese Jew. It was patronised by literary lions and royalty. The American poet Ezra

Pound and Wyndham Lewis, the 'Vorticists', celebrated the launch of their magazine *Blast* there in 1914. But regal favour was also extended to more modest eating-houses like the kosher salt-beef restaurant at 2 Charlotte Street run by the Kahn family. The proprietor's son Jack tells of how one day a man came in and ordered a kosher salt-beef sandwich. Mr Kahn asked the stranger if he would like mustard added. He said yes and Mr Kahn gave him the sandwich, for which the price was fourpence. The gentleman handed over half a crown. The shopkeeper bent down to find change but when he looked up to his surprise the man was gone. Mr Kahn rushed out of the shop to find him, and the doorman from the Eiffel Tower said, 'You know who that was don't you?'

'No,' replied the perplexed Mr Kahn.

'That was the Prince of Wales.'

After that he thought he should have been awarded the Royal Warrant.

Such was Judah's esteem in the local community that the Tavern was usually called 'Kleinfeld's' or just 'Klein's'. Even so, the Fitzroy could not have survived without his wife Jane. She was a short, plump lady who kept in the background of the pub. Her empire was upstairs, where they lived in extensive accommodation above the bars. In her domain she dispensed nosh and lemonade to the lucky children who visited. One such boy was Jack Itsbitsky, who lived opposite the Fitzroy at 4 Windmill Street, and another was 'Wolfie', the delivery boy for the kosher butcher Raznick. He would park his bike and bound up the stairs for reviving refreshment. Jane had a regular order of meat from Raznick, whose shop was just across the road at 37 Charlotte Street. Sometimes if she wanted something special she would send Annie over. This was one opportunity to leave the Tavern and she loved to chat to the other customers, most of whom she knew. Mr Raznick always stood behind the counter serving with his beaming friendly red face, almost the same colour as his blood-specked apron. Jane kept a strictly kosher home, and she was a true 'Yiddisher momma' determined to uphold her beliefs and keep the family going as far as was possible now they were running a tavern.

On Fridays the smells of Jane's cooking for the Sabbath were deliciously enticing – of onions and chicken fat being rendered down for schmaltz and the huge cauldron of chicken soup that sat simmering on the cooker for hours; then the added aroma of freshly fried fish wafted down to the bars below and mingled with the more familiar reek of beer, cigarette, pipe and cigar smoke to tantalise the customers. Many were privileged to partake of the Shabbat meal, like Dr Sidney Yale, the local Jewish medical practitioner and family friend whom Pop had first met when he employed him as the doctor for his Friendly Society. The novelist Louis Golding also recorded his appreciation for the lockshen soup he had sampled in one of the books he gave Annie.

Pop decided that with the pub's growing popularity, it needed livening up. One of the first improvements he made was to buy an electric pianola. It was a magnificent instrument adorned with lights on the front and pale pink shades trimmed with glass beads. It could be played by hand or with a penny in the slot. Annie couldn't help noticing that one man would come in day after day to put pennies in the machine. She became intrigued and at last she plucked up courage to ask him why. 'I'm Constant Lambert, the composer,' came the reply, 'and it gives me inspiration!' He lived in Percy Street and became a regular of the Fitzroy. The Irish composer E. J. Moeran also used to sit down on the piano stool to try out his compositions. If the piano could have talked like Sparky's, what amusing stories it would have told. Sometimes the penny stuck and the customer would bang on the box to shift it. The exasperated Pop would throw out the culprit who had done it on purpose to annoy him.

One day another customer brought Pop a set of recruiting posters from the First World War. He was delighted and had them framed. They would be just the thing to hang on the walls alongside the huge Victorian mirror. Soon the posters multiplied and quite transformed the stark interior of the bar. They were pictures by famous artists of the day like Dorothy Stanley and Hassel with such splendidly jingoistic titles as *The Women of Britain Say Go!, Is Your Country Worth Fighting For?, Save Us From the Hun!*, (ironically) *Save Serbia!, 1805 England Expects 1915 Are You Doing Your Duty Today?, Forward! Forward to*

Victory, *Enlist Now*, and of course Lord Kitchener's clarion call to arms, *Your Country Needs You.*

Another novel idea of Pop's dating from the early twenties originated when two men were playing darts in the public bar. This was where the real locals used to meet, and games like shove-ha'penny and darts were laid on for them. (Incidentally, Augustus John was a whizz at shove-ha'penny!) In a particularly competitive darts game, one customer became very frustrated when he lost, and threw his dart in the air. It lodged in the ceiling. Pop was in the bar at the time and heard the winner remark, 'That would be a good way to raise money for charity'. It gave Pop a brainwave and that night he wouldn't go to bed until he had perfected the scheme in his mind. He would invite customers to put money into coloured paper darts, which were then twisted up to hold the money and thrown onto the ceiling. From this inspired idea of Pop's the Fitzroy Money Box started, later to become the famous 'Pennies From Heaven'. The customers quickly took to this and contributed generously.

Annie and her father also introduced a loan club. To meet the costs of Christmas, customers were encouraged to save. Monday night was loan night and people would pay in anything from sixpence per week. A procession of old ladies in shawls and bonnets, old men – some with walrus moustaches – and a few younger folk lined up in the saloon bar to hand in their contributions to Annie, from the widow's mite up, who recorded the amounts in a special book. Annie did all the bookkeeping for the business, as in fact one of the main reasons Pop needed her help was that he could not write English. When they took over the Tavern she had been grateful for the friendly advice the Midland Bank manager had given her, and she again sought his help in setting up the club. The minimum amount saved by the customers would be 2s 6d. This was still enough to buy a bottle of whisky at Christmas or alternatively boxes of chocolates or jars of pickles.

Each week Annie would take the money to the Midland Bank for safe keeping. As pay out time approached, Annie would draw the money out of the bank on Friday and make up the pay-packets ready for the Monday hand-out. One year she had a problem – their dog went missing! Annie had a feeling it had been stolen and was uneasy about keeping the cash – some three thousand pounds – at the Fitzroy over the weekend, so she asked if the bank could open on Sunday for her to get the loan money out. Her friendly bank manager couldn't do this unheard of thing off his own bat but he agreed to ask head office. The reply came back that if he could find a volunteer, he could open the bank. To his surprise every member of staff offered to come in. So the Tottenham Court Road branch of the Midland Bank became the first bank to open on a Sunday. By a coincidence this branch had actually first opened in 1886, the year that Pop Kleinfeld came to London.

Nina Hamnett belonged to the club and used to encourage customers not only to save, but to give contributions for the ceiling collection and indeed buy her a drink! Nina would sit in the corner of the bar and sketch people as they queued to hand in their money. Annie was fascinated by the speed and deftness with which Nina worked in the brief moments as they shuffled past her. Though not her best, the results were still good enough for the front of each of the de luxe editions of her successful autobiography, *The Laughing Torso*, a 1930s best-seller in the UK and America. The 'torso' was Nina's; as a young art student she was described as having 'one of the most beautiful bodies in London' by Henri Gaudier-Brzeska. This talented but ill-fated artist became one of her many lovers and admirers and immortalised her in his statue *Torso of Nina*. He sculpted this from a piece of marble stolen from a stonemason's yard in Putney! It now stands in the Victoria and Albert Museum. She referred to this statue when she was first introduced to Ruthven Todd by Dylan Thomas, in the inimitable words, 'You know me, m'dear – I'm in the V&A with me left tit knocked off!'

Annie soon adapted to her role in the pub. One day a customer who had had rather too much to drink started to get fresh with her. She picked up a bottle and threw it at him. He needed several stitches. Annie felt dreadful but it was her only option. The next day he returned to apologise. She now put up her pigtails, grew in confidence and confessed the pub was a fine finishing-school. Annie made friends with many of the artistic patrons of the Fitzroy, particularly Nina, who at that time lived in rooms above L'Etoile restaurant. A great empathy developed between them in the early days. Nina watched with great interest as Annie matured from a teenager to a fine young woman and always remembered her birthday by giving her signed photos of herself to mark the occasion. One such dedication was *To Miss Kleinfeld in admiration of her amazing intellectual progress during the last six years. Nina Hamnett 12th Oct. 1931.*

One day Nina asked her, 'Have you an autograph book?' Annie confessed she hadn't, and so Nina promptly bought her one. This autograph book vividly reflected the artistic and literary clientele of the Tavern from 1927 to 1930. The customers not only signed their names but composed music, did sketches and wrote poetry. E. J. Moeran, the volatile Irish composer, scribbled eight bars of his *First Rhapsody*, while Peter Warlock (Philip Heseltine), Constant Lambert, Michael Birkbeck and Dennis Arnold all contributed some music. Artistically Nina set an example by sketching people drinking at the bar, and Geoffrey Nelson drew the 'snob windows'. But the most famous artist was undoubtedly Augustus John. He held up the album to the huge Victorian mirror and did a self-portrait in pen and ink. Another important artist was Christopher Richard Wynne Nevinson, the Vorticist and Futurist pioneer. He had a bulging forehead, flat nose and crinkly hair, which earned him the unfortunate nickname of 'Bucknigger'. Nevinson drew someone called Piggy in the book. There is also a good head-and-shoulders charcoal sketch of Pop himself. Other interesting drawings are Tony Powell's bar scene, Rowley Smart's rural life and the South African Roy Campbell captures the exhilaration of wild animals. Adrian Dainty outlined a young woman, and Chiquita, friend and model of Augustus John, signed a sketch of herself. Viva King the writer depicted her husband after a few drinks. Gwyn Evans, one of the top Sexton Blake authors, signed a picture of his supersleuth, adding 'with the accent on sex'.

The sex object of the Fitzroy, however, undoubtedly was Betty May, the fiery model of the sculptor Jacob Epstein. Not only was she portrayed in drawings, but her host of male admirers extolled her in verse. Powys Mathers dedicated a poem to her entitled *Oh, That We Two Were Betty Maying*. He describes Betty round him 'like a drunk confetti' and ends by asking Pop for a 'double and a splash'. Betty herself neatly wrote:

> Kleinfeld's kind I'm glad to say,
> Sometimes I owe, sometimes I pay,
> But whoever does,

Betty May
July 1928

That same month Betty had a brief affair with the Australian, Jack Lindsay. Jack and his friend, P. R. 'Inky' Stephenson, were two boys from Queensland who took on the London literary scene between 1927 and 1929, running the Fanfrolico Press in Bloomsbury. They found the Fitzroy a most welcoming pub to repair to after their literary labours, with the merry and mellow Judah, aided by the coy Annie, behind the bar. 'Inky' exuded infectious gaiety and would burst into the Fitzroy, demanding drinks all round. 'Then there would be back-slapping, laughter, excitement that seemed to tinkle thrillingly along the very glasses on the shelves. He stirred a pub to life.' (Philip Lindsay in *I'd Live the Same Life Over*). Jack, with his striking black beard would join in the fun and the pair would energetically drink the foaming Toby ale, which they topped up with over-proof Jerusalem brandy. Jack and 'Inky' epitomised the boisterous atmosphere of this Bohemian Tavern in the late twenties. Jack not only linked his signature with Betty May's in Annie's autograph book, but also penned this amusing little ditty:

> Here be liquors, all drinks handy
> Even to Jerusalem Brandy –
> Far have I drunk and widely spewed
> In roaring parties, in solitude,
> But seldom have I quite so fine felt
> As at odd moments served by Kleinfeldt.

Jack Lindsay
August 31st 1928

The 'Kleinfelts' were regarded in apt tributes from old habitués: *to Kleinfeld and Annie, for providing an oasis of joy in a desert of boredom, the most congenial hosts in London* and *best of friends.* Fellow restaurateurs felt the same way about Judah.

SKETCHES FROM ANNIE'S AUTOGRAPH BOOK

after a few drinks →

Portrait of my husband.

F S King

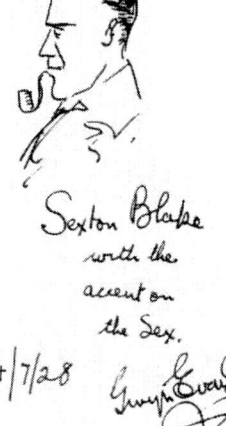

Sexton Blake
with the
accent on
the Sex.

4/7/28

Gwyn Evans

1929.

BETTY MAY

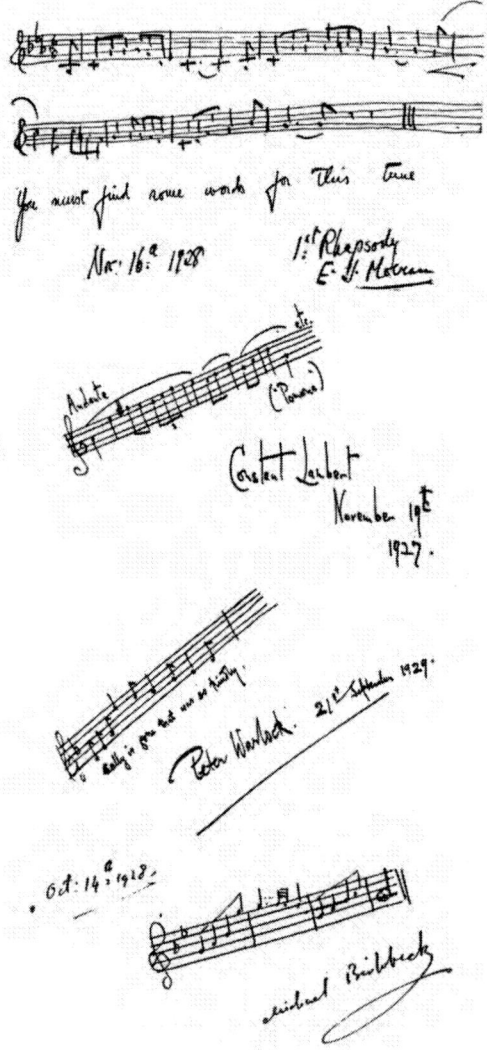

You must find some words for this tune

Nov: 16th 1928   1st Rhapsody
                                  E. J. Moeran

Andante   (Piano)

Constant Lambert
November 19th
1927.

really in grave but not so trying.

Peter Warlock.   21st September 1929.

Oct: 14th 1928.

Michael Birchbeck

Ich leibe Kleinfeld, wrote Rudolf Stulik. In fact there was only one grievance, in the whole album:

> Whether I come at night or noon
> I've only one complaint – It's always Time too soon.

Perhaps the most succinct and apt two-liner came from Patrick Kirwan in February 1929:

> Annexe to the Temple of the Muses
> Where, musing done, the poet boozes.

This summed up the Fitzroy of this period admirably.

The range of literary entries was very wide. Donald Calthrop, who starred in the film *Blackmail*, the first 'talkie' in this country, directed by Alfred Hitchcock, wrote an amusing limerick:

> There was a young fellow called Throp
> Kept his friends very much 'on the hop',
> For the question was vext
> 'What would he do next?'
> Be a devil, a saint, or a FLOP?

Equally witty was the greeting, *To all Mariners – particularly Naval mariners and especially good 'Buntings' and 'Sparkers' (among whom I was once a Queen Bee). Have a crack at the Ceiling! Kaspar – 23rd May 1929.* This is probably Augustus John's son, who became an admiral.

Two substantial poems should be quoted in full. On 21st November 1919 Tommy Earp wrote:

> *On Being Asked To Write In This Album*

> When thus commanded by Miss K.,

Who would not rack his brains the harder,
Her gracious order to obey
With equal promptitude and ardour?

But how can any words avail,
From mere mortals such as me be,
Appropriately to state and hail
The glory of the goddess Hebe?

Were it not better but to raise,
With tongue-tied reverence and emotion,
An elbow in her heartfelt praise,
And toast her in an amber ocean?

An equally witty poem was written by Professor J. B. Haldane, the brilliant but controversial scientist, geneticist and broadcaster. His entry reflects the wide range of talented artists that might be encountered on entering the Fitzroy.

On entering Mr Kleinfeld's portal
One may well find oneself immortal,
For I only have to whistle
To have my portrait done by Bissell,
And if he does not do me justice
I take a sitting with Augustus.
If I prefer my artist heavy
I ooze around and sit with Nevvy,
Whilst if I like them somewhat leaner
I run away and pose for Nina.
And my phiz will decorate
The Louvre, the Prado, and the Tate.

His wife Charlotte had given Annie a different religious dedication, *Mazeltov to Annie, whose eyes shine as brightly as Chanucah candles. From her co-religionist.* Charlotte was an author in her own right and wrote *Brother to Bert.* Another woman who wrote in the book was Mary Butts, a Bohemian friend of Nina's from Paris days:

Home Again ENGLAND –

Two dolphins on Trinity House:
Two danish tug-boats:
Magnus Martyn's white & gold.
WINDSOR –
Mary Queen of Scots, Caroline Lamb – round & back again
– to all the new boys & girls in Mr Kleinfeld's Bar –

Mary Butts
25.9.28

Barbara Higgins described the delight of an ice-floe as it moved towards the Equator, 'In the mood of the ice when it melts/Come to Kleinfelt's!', while Nancy Cunard, the social butterfly who patronised the Café Royal, wrote that she had looked for Michael Roberts – in vain, on 10th February. This amusing entry was capped by A. H. Mahony, who basked in the glory of actually writing in the book. He had 'at last achieved fame by being asked by Miss K. to write in her album'.

Apart from Augustus John, the most famous artistic patron of the Fitzroy, often accompanied by his models, was Jacob Epstein. The outstanding sculptor of his time, he was a tempestuous and controversial character and his models were even more so! One was Dolores, a fine subject for any artist with her black hair, splendid profile and white face, which contrasted vividly with the black dress she almost always wore. Nina would take her home and do several sketches which she said where 'a good likeness but not good drawings'. They would work for four to five hours and then visit the Fitzroy for much needed refreshment. Dolores would argue and sometimes come to blows with Epstein's other model, the redoubtable Betty May.

Betty was nicknamed 'Tiger Woman', on account of her wild-cat temperament. She was tiny but her angelic appearance belied her violent nature. Those green eyes could blaze with savage ferocity and woe betide the victim of her wrath. She dressed like a gypsy and delighted in shocking people. Her favourite cabaret act at the Fitzroy was to squat on all fours and drink from a saucer, to the hilarity for all. As noted in the autograph book, she had an enormous male fan club. Men were obsessed with her 'pantherine' movements and flashing eyes. One such slave was the young Oxford graduate Raoul Loveday, who Betty married. He died tragically in bizarre circumstances after being initiated into occultism. Interest in the occult was another ingredient in the spicy Bohemian Fitzrovian stew. The high priest of Satanism was Aleister Crowley. Though he was a customer at the Fitzroy, his presence was not encouraged by Annie as he was a dangerous man. He did contribute to Annie's autograph book, and in September 1941 he was to give her a signed copy, No. 89, out of the 100 copies that were printed of his book *Thumbs Up*, *a pentagram and pantacle to win the war*. The dedication was *To my good friend Annie with sincere affection.* Denise Hooker describes him as a 'megalomaniac with a talent for self-dramatisation'. Devotees would indulge in the Rites of Eleusis, worshipping Pan at the Abbey of Thelema in Sicily, which Crowley and his mistress, the Scarlet Woman, would preside over. Against the advice of Nina, Betty May took Raoul to Cefalu, where he died at the Abbey from enteritis after allegedly drinking a cat's blood as part of some ritual sacrifice.

This orgiastic fatality had a dramatic legal consequence. Nina Hamnett in her book *Laughing Torso* mentioned that the Crowley practised black magic at Cefalu and that one day a baby vanished mysteriously. Crowley, against advice, started libel proceedings against Nina, her publishers, Constable & Co., and the printers in 1934. The trial before Mr Justice Swift was a *cause célébre* which was manna to the avid press. Crowley lost the case, of course, but Betty May was called as defence witness and under cross-examination she admitted that much of Nina's autobiography was fabrication from the ghost writing of Gilbert Armitage. Naturally after this the friendship between Nina and Betty cooled considerably!

But the Fitzroy was to witness an amusing sequel, as recalled by the poet Ruthven Todd in the catalogue introduction to *Fitzrovia & The Road to the York Minster.*

Once morning when I happened to have a little money on me, I bought one of the less restrained morning papers and, shortly after opening time, I went to the Fitzroy. Nina was ahead of me, sitting by the fire with a drink in her hand. I sat on a stool by the bar and sipped at my half of bitter while I glanced at the paper. On the third page there was a dingy photo, but my eye caught...the caption: 'Miss Nina Hamnett, the artist and author of *Laughing Torso*, takes a walk in the Park with a friend'. I looked more closely at the not too clear...reproduction and started to chortle. 'Nina,' I called out, 'You MUST see this. It's damn funny.' She came over...and concentrated on the figure. It was unmistakenly of Betty May with an unidentified man. 'Have you half-a-crown you can lend for an hour or so, m'dear?'...and, obediently, I produced the needed coin. 'And can I borrow your paper?' I passed that over too. Nina left the Fitzroy with her erect but odd bustling walk and, looking out after her, I saw her grab a taxi. I don't think she was gone more than three-quarters of an hour. 'Here's your half-crown and paper back, m'dear.' I looked at her with expression of surprise and saw that she was delighted with herself. 'I went to Fleet Street, m'dear, and told them, they'd libelled me. They settled for twenty-five quid, m'dear, and I signed a release for them. Drink up, m'dear, and have a better drink.'

Annie, who was behind the bar, was delighted for Nina's good fortune, as twenty-five pounds in those days was a lot of money, and so was everyone in the bar when Nina announced, 'The drinks are on me.' But Annie's glee soon turned to worry when Betty May stalked in. Trouble, thought Annie – there'll be fireworks. But to Betty's astonishment Nina handed her the double whisky she herself had just ordered. When Betty realised the score, she also borrowed Ruthven Todd's half-crown and grabbed his paper. She ran out of the bar, shouting, 'I've been libelled too.' She also returned triumphant and told how the beleagured paper had coughed up another twenty-five quid. The newspaper didn't want to get involved with a person of Betty's reputation as she was not called 'Tiger Woman' for nothing! The party went on all day and generous donations were thrown onto the Fitzroy ceiling by the two ladies. Betty May in her autobiography appropriately entitled *Tiger Woman* wrote, 'There is nowhere quite like the Fitzroy. It seems more of a café than a public house as anything I know in England. Its proprietor Mr Kleinfeld and his charming daughter Annie are some of the nicest and kindest people I know and I am sure there lots of people like me who feel they could not do without them.'

Annie, like her father, helped many customers such as Gwyn Evans, the creator of the Sexton Blake comic strip. The son of a Welsh Archdruid, he was one of a team of six who met to record the inexhaustible adventures of Sexton Blake and his youthful assistant, Tinker. By 1930 he reckoned that he had sold over two million words about the supersleuth. Annie had long discussions with him and always tried to encourage him to write books, as she felt he could do much better. He persevered with his writing and was truly grateful to Annie for her faith in him. When his book, *Mr Hercules*, a more serious shocker, was published, he dedicated a copy to Annie: *To Ann because she believed.*

Another regular befriended by Annie was George Mitcheson. George was standing as prospective Member of Parliament for St Pancras South and Annie did all she could to help get him accepted. She invited him to old folks and childrens Christmas parties and her efforts increased during the run-up to the 1931 general election. On , she sent George a white heather horseshoe for good luck, which he had mounted on the front of his car. George was successful and thanked Annie profusely afterwards for the inspiration and good work she had done for his campaign.

Politics was always a rich vein at the Fitzroy and many others went on to make their name on the political stage from humble beginnings. One of these was Sir Charles Irving. Charles first came to the Fitzroy when working the old Cavendish Hotel at the end of the rule of the formidable Rosa Lewis, the 'Duchess of Jermyn Street'. He recalled that at this time he was earning something like one pound a week. He was but one to receive Judah Kleinfeld's generosity. Sir Charles later had a most distinguished career as MP for Cheltenham, but he never forgot the friends he made at the Fitzroy and the parties there. He described the Fitzroy as an oasis of pleasure and education with always a warm welcome and personal kindness.

Annie, as a relaxation from all her hard work at the Fitzroy, became interested in quite a different activity – flying! A number of pilots and navigators used to come into the pub from Alan Cobham's 'Flying Circus'. One of these called Ross took a shine to Annie and persuaded her to go flying with them. She loved the exhilaration and excitement of it, and even went up in open planes, not strapped in, gaining a certificate for looping the loop. These magnificent men in their flying machines made such an impression on Annie that she organised parties of customers to go with her and Ross to Hendon Aerodrome. Ross was in charge of a special van with a huge loudspeaker on top to announce the programme of displays for the circus. It used to blare out the music of Irving Berlin in time to the stunts of the planes. Annie's great delight was when the planes used to drop mock bombs of flour onto the audience. This enjoyable pastime stopped for Annie when the Circus left for South Africa, and Annie received a telegram saying *Cheerio Ross*. Annie always looked back on that cryptic note as a premonition of disaster, for the next thing she heard was that there had been a tragic accident on 17th February 1933. During one of the displays Captain Lawson and Ross had been killed. Annie was heartbroken. But life had to go on and soon romance was to blossom for her again.

3

Annie and the Guv

Later that year Annie accompanied her father on their annual Derby Day outing. Pop would hire a coach, which he filled with booze to take him and a party of customers to Epsom. On this wonderful day out Pop was amazed by a very tall man in spectacular African chieftain's robes and feathered head-dress who loudly proclaimed to racegoers, 'I've gotta Horse, I've gotta Horse'. This flamboyant racing tout called himself the Zulu Prince Monolulu. He surprised Pop soon afterwards by flinging open the Tavern doors and in full regalia uttering his famous cry to the astounded company. He had a variety of multicoloured satin jackets, some of green and gold and one decorated with horseshoes, four-leaf clover and winning-posts. Although he claimed to be an African prince, his real name was Peter McKay and he lived in Cleveland Street. Peter really was one of the most colourful Fitzrovian characters and is nostalgically remembered today in the pub named after him in Fitzroy Street.

However, Annie's attention that Derby Day was focused on their coach-driver, a very good-looking Jewish boy named Charles Allchild. Charles' family had come from Russia and settled in the East End of London. Though most of his brothers had taken up tailoring, Charlie trained as a motor-mechanic. Annie and Charles fell in love and on Midsummer's Day, 24th June 1934, the wedding was solemnised in the Masonic Temple of the Princes' Gallery, Piccadilly, under the special canopy (the chuppah) which had been taken from the synagogue and erected specially in the Temple. It was a splendid wedding with 600 guests. The nine-course banquet had whole pigeons as the main delicacy, all laid on by J. Sterns, the kosher caterers. The guest list read like a *Who's Who* of the Jewish West End community. Guests included many friends and colleagues from the West End

Great Synagogue, and even Augustus John was there. The local police hired high hats for the occasion. Bernard Levin wrote in later years, 'The guests ranged from a Cabinet Minister to a roadsweeper. There in brief was the whole story of the Fitzroy.' Pop had seen to it that the local sweep should be there to wish Annie and Charles good luck, a romantic and caring fatherly gesture. The music at the wedding was played by the talented coloured jazz musician Rudolph Dunbar, a Fitzroy regular. Rudolph had begun his career as a jazz pianist in cabaret, then changed to classical and became the first black conductor of the London Philharmonic Orchestra at the Albert Hall. This occasion, he confided to Annie, had almost overawed him when he saw the audience filling the Albert Hall from floor to ceiling.

F. S. Matta, wine distributors to the Tavern, gave them the use of the Castello Bellagrino for their honeymoon in Venice. The castle had a romantic setting in a vast vineyard and was the perfect place for an idyllic interlude. With further generosity Mr Matta presented the pair with a rare magnum of Napoleon champagne cognac. Another present was a canteen of cutlery from Desio Vaiani and a group of Fitzrovians called 'The Fitzroy Circle'. This honeymoon was to be their only holiday for the rest of their time in the Fitzroy.

When they returned from Venice they made the Tavern their home. Charles helped in the running of the pub and was a very handy man. He always spoke in rhyming slag from his East End upbringing and he would delight to tell the customers, 'Shut that Rory O'More' (the door) or the potman Harry to 'go down the apples and pears' (stairs) to see to the beer. Pop Kleinfeld saw how the customers liked his son-in-law and he felt he would be ideal as mine host of the Tavern. So Jane and Judah decided to bow out gracefully and retire. By law, a lady couldn't hold a licence solely; accordingly Annie and Charles became joint licensees and tenants.

The Kleinfelds moved to Hove, but still kept an interest in the Fitzroy. Every Sunday morning Pop would return to the pub, where he would sit on his special stool in the saloon bar, handing out small cigars to all his friends. Many of them were the local Jewish tailors who had just collected their pay. They were still wearing their high hats, which was customary when they went to receive their wages. Their usual tipple was half-quarters, a triple measure of spirits, and Pop would happily chat with them and other customers catching up on all the news and gossip.

But soon after the old generation of the family departed, there was a new addition. Happy domestic news arrived in the shape of a baby girl on 4th May 1936, delivered by Dr Yale at 5.30 a.m. in the second floor main bedroom of the Fitzroy. She was named Sally Thelma and thus was definitely Fitzroy born and bred – a pure Fitzrovian. What excitement there was in the bars when they opened up that morning. Part of the top floor of the Fitzroy was turned into a special nursery suite and a nanny was employed to look after Sally, and a trusty and kindly maid Esther was engaged. Sally's first 'public' appearance was when she emerged from the Tavern doors aged twelve weeks, sleeping in her mother's arms to the deafening rendition of Gracie Field's *Sally* by the children off on the annual outing to Boxmoor. Later that afternoon she perked up, to help Annie give a bouquet to Lady Mitcheson, who presented the children with prizes. When Sally was two years old Norah James dedicated her latest novel to her. The book was called *The House by the Tree* and the inscription read: *To Sally hoping that one day she herself will write a much better book and dedicate it to me.*

As Sally grew up, she started to investigated the nooks and crannies of the Fitzroy. She watched fascinated as her mother sat doing the books in the office, and a world of wonderment opened up when her father unlocked the special cupboard where he kept his stocks of cigarettes, cigars and matches. The room was filled with a familiar pungent aroma. The cigarettes were set out in rows – Wills, Gold Flake, Players, Craven "A" and Passing Cloud (the bright pink being her favourite colour). It was a special treat for Sally to replenish the shelf behind the saloon bar from the cupboard, a task that had to be performed before opening.

As both Charles and Annie smoked heavily, Charles saved and collected cigarette-cards and even the wrapping strips of cigars. He was an inveterate hoarder and kept foreign stamps and bank-notes. One that gave him a particular thrill was a one-pound note with the number 1,000,000 on it. 'That's the nearest I'll get to a million,' Charlie used to say. His other delight was to make cheese sandwiches every day. These were the only food that was provided at the Fitzroy. Sally couldn't work out how he made a piece of Cheddar cheese go so far. The sandwiches were cut to perfection with the exact amount of finely sliced strips of cheese, and were always sold out each day at sixpence a round.

The Fitzroy, as with most of the other pubs in the area, was essentially for the sale of alcohol, not food, as hardened drinkers like Nina Hanmett and Augustus John could verify. Another devotee of the amber nectar at the Fitzroy and elsewhere was Dylan Thomas. Augustus John, in *Finishing Touches*, remembered his first meeting with Dylan, which happened to be in the Fitzroy. On that particular evening the Tavern was particularly crowded. Professor Haldane, seeming oblivious to the noise, was deep in thought, notebook in hand. As Augustus took his seat he heard above the din 'the somewhat blurred but no less authoritative accents of South Wales'. It was, of course, Dylan of tubby figure, round face, red hair and 'slightly sardonic smile'. To a native of the same Welsh county, his voice came across with a beautiful resonance, the 'best English in Carmarthenshire'. Immediately there were drinks all round and Dylan was the life and soul of the party. The only trouble was that when he had consumed a few too many, the Welsh magic departed and only the 'interminable reverberations of the alcoholic' were left. Augustus personally felt that possibly his 'grassiest verses originated in the fetid atmosphere' of pubs like the Fitzroy. It was a fact that he left his only copy of *Under Milk Wood* after a drinking session at The York Minster, latterly The French House. Several times Annie had to throw Dylan out of the Fitzroy, though at this time his drink was still beer. Only when he went to America did he indulge heavily in spirits, which led to his untimely death.

While the Fitzroy remained the 'headquarters' for the faithful like Nina and Augustus, the surrounding pubs all had attractions for serious Fitzrovian topers. The hard core of pubs were the Black Horse, Bricklayers Arms, Wheatsheaf, Marquis of Granby, Duke of York and the Beer House, apart from nearby Soho watering-holes like the Highlander, York Minster, Swiss and Half Past Two House. A pub-crawl was an essential part of the Fitzrovian ritual and was a well-timed affair, according to the Ceylonese poet J. M. Tambimuttu. Everyone got to know where they could find each other at any time of the day or evening even before or after normal pub hours since nightclubs, restaurants and cafés were 'beads in the smoky necklace of the pub-crawl'. Contrary to the popular belief, Bohemians, although they professed a healthy contempt for the conventional, within their own parameters were very conservative.

So in the morning they met at Madame Buhler's in Charlotte Street for coffee to clear the head after the previous evening's excesses before starting again at the nearest pub. Of these Fitzrovian pubs, the Black Horse, Rathbone Place, with its Tudor façade, was a serious competitor to the Fitzroy. Its celebrity turn came on punctually at six every evening when Mrs Stewart entered. She was an elderly lady swathed in black who, over her glass of Guinness and in between doing two crosswords, could reel out anecdotes on virtually every subject. Across the road from the Wheatsheaf was the more rough-and-ready Marquis of Granby, patronised by a shadier clientele. Further along, the Duke of York had an amazing proprietor, Major Alf Klein. From time to time he would dress up and ride the streets in a pony and trap. He was nicknamed the 'Mad Major'. But perhaps the most unusual pub was the so-called 'Beer House'. As its name suggests it supplied only beer, in a one-room bar. Tambimuttu felt it was sensible to repair there later in the evening, when the major pubs were overflowing, to find the bar relatively empty and enjoy a quiet pint of ale. The finale of the pub-crawl came at 10.30 p.m., when the Fitzroy and Wheatsheaf stopped serving alcohol in line with Holborn licensing laws. This ensured a dash across Charlotte Street to the Marquis of Granby and Duke of York, which, being in Marylebone, shut at 11 p.m. Jack Kahn remembers sitting in his room and hearing the sound of stampeding feet as the crowd made their mad rush across the street.

This pub-crawl was but one facet of the Fitzrovian mystique, as described by Tambimuttu. 'Tambi' was the editor of *Poetry London* and it was he who coined the phrase 'Sohoitis'. He warned a young writer, Julian MacLaren-Ross, after a particularly heavy drinking bout, 'Only beware of Fitzrovia...It's a dangerous place, you must be careful.'

'Fights with knives?'

'No, a worse danger. You might get Sohoitis, you know.'

'No I don't. What is it?'

'If you get Sohoitis,' Tambi said very seriously, 'you will stay there always day and night and get no work done ever. You have been warned.'

The name stuck from that day!

Tambi captured that quintessential atmosphere of Fitzrovia in the period immediately before the Second World War. He first came to London in 1938 and initially settled at 45 Howland Street, before moving to a flat in Whitfield Street. Tambi had a distinctive appearance; long black hair surrounded his lazy almond-shaped face. His favourite ploy was to go round customers in the bar with a borrowed hat and importune with his simian double-jointed fingers for money for his impecunious friend, a struggling artist. When he judged his hat was full enough, he deftly pocketed the proceeds and ordered drinks all round. Grudgingly he allowed his companion half a pint for his pains!

Charles Haddon Redvers Gray was the first English Bohemian that Tambi encountered – in the Harem nightclub. Haddon led a nomadic existence. By day he would ride his rusty bike, play the flute in the street and squat in the lotus position in Tambi's flat. Other poets like Stephen Spender and Philip O'Connor came to Tambi's memorable parties. Beautiful ladies graced his flat, like Anaïs Nin and Mary Hunt, adored by Augustus John and Matthew Smith. Another attractive young woman would parade up and down naked in the building opposite the flat, quite unconcerned although she knew that all the men were watching her every move. Those were the days! To Tambi, Fitzrovians were vagabonds, sadhakers or seekers, as earlier suggested by William J. Locke's *'The Beloved Vagabond'* and also in the lines of Lord Byron, *'So we'll go no more a-roving by the light of the moon.'*

And so it was that this golden age of the Fitzroy drew to a close. The times they were a-changing. A new influx of people were to discover the Fitzroy while, on a wider scale, the storm clouds in Europe were gathering. Armageddon was about to be unleashed on London. The Fitzroy could not escape and so the happy family life there was bound to be interrupted by the outbreak of war. Though Sally had to be evacuated with her nanny and housekeeper to Somerset, Charles and Annie decided that the Fitzroy must stay open if possible and do its duty for Fitzrovia and Londoners.

4

Fitzrovia Does Its Duty

Charles and Annie responded in true Nelsonian fashion to the war challenge by adopting a ship, particularly as it was called HMS *Fitzroy*. It was so named after Vice Admiral Robert Fitzroy, son of Lord Charles Fitzroy. Admiral Fitzroy as a younger man had commanded the *Beagle* on which Darwin sailed on his famous survey to the Galapagos Islands in 1831 to 1836. In later life he fell out with Darwin when the naturalist put forward his Theory of Evolution, and committed suicide by cutting his throat on Sunday morning, 30th April 1865. Charlie in any event had been negotiating to buy the ship's bell because the ship was going to be broken up. But when war was declared, HMS *Fitzroy* was reprieved and commissioned for war use under the Lend-Lease scheme. She slipped down the ways at her US shipyard, a mere eight and half days after her keel had been relaid, a record for building a minesweeper. The revamped HMS *Fitzroy*, skippered by Commander A. C. Duckworth, proudly entered the war as part of the Fourth Flotilla of Minesweepers. The customers at the Fitzroy wholeheartedly supported the adoption, and they followed with interest the ship's operations in the Channel. A special box was placed on the bar counter for contributions and people gave generously despite wartime stringencies. So the Fitzroy was stunned by the terrible news that, after the gallant crew had completed twenty-nine successful trips, the ship had been torpedoed. Then a few days after came the welcome telegram, 'Boarding you tonight – HMS *Fitzroy*'.

It transpired that the ship had been hit in very shallow waters with no loss of life. The Commander, who later received the D.S.O. for his bravery, also managed to save the name-plate and white ensign. These he handed over to Annie to resounding cheers in the presence of the entire ship's company, plus crew from her sister ships HMS *Kellet* and HMS *Speedwell* when they descended on the Fitzroy that evening. The sailors in turn took off their cap tallies and presented them to Annie, which all added to the growing collection of war memorabilia. The Fitzroy was beginning to look like a war museum! It was quite a party that night. Drinks were on the house for the lads and few escaped hangovers the next morning.

Cap tally collecting had started after the scuttling of the 'unsinkable' German pocket battleship *Graf Spee* off Montevideo in the River Plate on 17th December 1939, after a bombardment of shells from the *Ajax, Exeter* and *Achilles*. Bruce Belfrage, the BBC newsreader and Fitzroy customer, had triumphantly announced that night to the world that 'the German 'PACKET BOTTLESHIP, the *Graf Spee*,' was no more. Bruce never forgot this dramatic public *faux pas*, which he often brought up in conversations afterwards in the pub with Annie. After a stirring victory parade in London held on the ships' return, many of the sailors made their way that evening to the Fitzroy and a member of each crew gave Annie a cap tally. Eventually this unique collection had tallies not only from the Royal Navy but the Australian, Canadian, Dutch, Swedish, French and Indian navies.

Though HMS *Fitzroy* had been sunk, the Tavern was determined to adopt another ship. When an American Liberty ship was named *Fitzroy,* to keep the sailors warm, Annie and a group of customers decided to knit balaclavas, socks, scarves and mittens for the crew from special oiled wool, supplied by Annie. One of these knitting helpers was James Norbury, known to the Tavern regulars as Roy. He was a lifelong friend of Nina's and worked for Patons and Baldwins Ltd as their chief knitting designer and historian.

One young sailor who used to visit the Fitzroy at this time and who was befriended by Annie was Carl. He lived in Albany Street and looked on Annie as a sort of adoptive mother. Carl was serving on a ship called HMS *Whitney Bay* and Annie collected crates of books for him so that a ship's library could be started. Though Carl never had much literary interest, he was put in charge and slaved away to organise the library. The books brought brief moments of relaxation during the terrible times at sea until a near-miss bomb settled the ship at the bottom of the sea off the Dutch coast. The books, however, were stored in steel cupboards and would probably remain in good condition for ever in Davy Jones' locker, so Carl assured Annie.

All this patriotic morale-boosting by the Fitzroy did not pass unnoticed by another regular, the young journalist Tom Driberg. As Annie glanced through her *Daily Express* just before opening on Wednesday 27th March 1940, she saw the headline 'NO MOANING AT THIS BAR'. To her surprise she realised the article was all about the Fitzroy! It explained how the Tavern had adopted a ship, the first time a pub had ever done this, and gave much more information about this unique hostelry. More importantly, for the first time William Hickey, the columnist, had officially called the surrounding district Fitzrovia because its central shrine was the Fitzroy Tavern. As Annie and Charles digested this, they guessed that 'William Hickey' was none other than Tom Driberg, the first person to write under this pseudonym.

To help morale further, Annie and Charles produced many special visiting-cards, which they handed out to customers. As the Blitz hit London and there was a complete blackout, the Fitzroy never closed, the atmosphere was electric and money continued to be thrown on the ceiling. Carl remembered one awful night when the bombing was intense. The explosions and gunfire rose in a crescendo but so did the defiant singing inside. Carl always kept his eyes on the steel tables under which everybody dived for protection. When the 'all-clear' sounded, Annie handed Carl the visiting-card, which he kept. On the reverse it read *It won't be long now V...*

The London Blitz did, however, hit Charles personally. Charles was very proud of his car at that time – a bright-red Pontiac which he called his 'fire-engine'. He mainly used it to drive down to Somerset and would brag to his customers how he could do the journey door-to-door in four hours. On his favourite stretch of road where it was straight for over a mile, he could put his food down and the 'fire-engine' would speed along at 100 m.p.h. Ironically, the car's nickname proved most apt, for when not in use, he garaged it at Jackson's Garage in Rathbone Place. As the Blitz intensified, the authorities requisitioned the garage for a temporary sub-fire station. The ground floor housed fire appliances, the basement served as a waiting area and mess-room for the firemen, and the floors above, reached by a lift, stored cars.

On 17th September 1940, one of the worst nights of the Blitz, a high explosive crashed through the roof of the garage, demolishing the entire building including Charlie's prized automobile. Charles was devastated, but a consolation was the bravery shown by young Harry Errington, the son of one of his friends. Harry was a volunteer auxiliary fireman and, as the family lived in Rathbone Place, he was assigned to work from Jackson's Garage. That awful night Harry's courageous actions in saving two of his colleagues from the building were to earn him the nation's highest bravery award, the George Cross. In fact he was the only London fire-fighter to be thus honoured and the pride felt for him and his family within the local Jewish community was tremendous.

Sally, of course, missed all the excitement of the Blitz safe in the Somerset village of Baltensbrough. Charles himself was eventually called up in 1941 to the RAF. This left Annie on her own with a loyal skeleton staff which included her cousin Sid Kleinfield. 'Pop' again jointly held the licence with Annie because of the rule against sole women licensees. Annie held the fort bravely but her worst moments were when she had to go down to the cellars to 'fine down' the beer. The rats were disturbed by the bombings and to Annie's horror she would often be aware of them watching her work. In time she became quite used to these rodent spectators, which she called her 'friends'. At least they kept her company.

Annie coped pretty well and was proud that she never had to call the police to sort out trouble. She was diplomatic if people had too much to drink, and with the help of stalwart Fitzrovians was able to eject the most difficult inebriates. On one rare occasion she experienced anti-Semitism. Charles' eldest brother Dick had been bombed out and had come to live at the Tavern. As a bachelor, he used to go to clubs like the Albany and Eccentric and one of his friends was a member of the aristocracy. This noble lord accompanied Dick to the Fitzroy one night and got plastered. When Annie politely asked him to leave, he viciously retorted, 'Take your filthy Jewish hands off me.' At this point Annie propelled him outside at speed. A few weeks later, the nobleman asked Dick if his sister had forgiven him. 'Never,' said Dick, 'and don't try to go there again.'

Charles was first sent to RAF Bridlington, where there were no uniforms to fit his huge bulk – at this time he weighed about eighteen stone. The same problem faced the corporal in charge of stores at Northolt when he was moved there. Being such a large, impressive man with a congenial personality he was often in the early days mistaken for the C.O. At his next posting, Bradwell Bay, he was actually billeted in the grounds of Bradwell Lodge, Kent, the home of Tom Driberg, and by a further coincidence he met Squadron Leader Ralph Reader who, with the RAF Gang Show, was entertaining the troops. They chatted about the Fitzroy, the money on the ceiling and the Children's Outings, and on his next visit to London Ralph visited the Tavern. This was the start of a close friendship between Annie and Ralph. For the remainder of his RAF service, Charles was at Uxbridge, which enabled him to return on leave to help Annie. His RAF career ended in 1943 when he was discharged on the grounds of ill health because of his excess weight. He had at least attained the rank of sergeant.

But 1943 was also a sad year for Annie as her mother Jane died aged seventy-nine. Pop was devastated by the loss of his lifelong partner, and as soon as possible he was to move back to London to 100 Ivor Court near Baker Street, so he could be near the Fitzroy. Concerned to keep her family together, Annie whenever she could brought Sally back to London and the Tavern for brief visits.

On one such night the Fitzroy was very busy. Charles was in the bar, while Annie and Sally were in the kitchen. Suddenly Annie froze as she was about to hand Sally a drink. The familiar piercing banshee wail of the air-raid siren had started. There was no time to get to the shelter, so routinely she dragged Sally into the passage at the back of the Tavern where there were no windows. As they clung to each other, they could hear the eerie whistling of the doodlebug getting louder by the second. She put her arms round Sally even tighter and as she did, the noise stopped. 'Oh God,' she prayed, 'I hope this one's not for us!' Then after what seemed like an eternity, it landed with a deafening thud. The whole building shook and the noise of breaking windows and falling debris was terrifying. Everything went quiet and Annie thanked God they were alive and the Fitzroy as still standing.

Annie and her daughter went cautiously downstairs, to hear the customers singing in full voice in the bars, as they always did during raids. Charles was exclaiming patriotically, 'We're not going to be defeated.' Miraculously, despite the blast and all the windows being blown in, not a glass or bottle was broken, not one packet of money fell from the ceiling and no one had been hurt. But outside it was very different. The bomb had landed next door, literally cutting off adjacent buildings and demolishing four houses. The damage was immense – the house a few doors away, No. 38 with its wonderful grapevine which had become a feature of Windmill Street, was a pile of rubble.

As Annie took in the full scale of the tragedy, she was aware of something touching her foot. She looked down and there on the doorstep was the smallest black kitten she had ever seen. Annie promptly picked it up, saying it was a good luck omen. Annie felt the same way about the money on the ceiling and resisted customers' requests to take it down. It became one of the wartime myths that people were safe in the Fitzroy bars with the money above them. But they were more reassured by the large steel tables that could cover them during an air raid.

Another eyewitness of this raid was Millicent Davies, whose father had a trimming shop in Windmill Street next door to the Fitzroy. She ran out into the street with her father when the bomb was dropping and stayed on the pavement. Millicent vividly remembers one unusual side-effect of the raid. The dray horses stabled at the Hooper Struve brewery broke loose and stampeded across Charlotte Street into Goodge Street, ending up in Catesby's furniture shop in Tottenham Court Road. She was nearly killed in their mad gallop,. They were eventually rounded up by the frantic 'cowboys'. So the Fitzroy, like St Paul's, seemingly inviolate and unshaken by the aerial bombardment of Goering's Luftwaffe, carried on throughout the war.

The collection of war souvenirs multiplied and attracted people from every corner of the globe. Second World War posters supplemented the First World War ones with the catch-phrases of the day to stiffen the nation's resolve against Hitler. They had such memorable titles as *'Dig for victory', 'Don't help the enemy! Careless talk may give away vital secrets'* (Fougassen), *'Three words to the whole nation – Go to it'* (Herbert Morrison), *'Hitler will send no warning – So always carry your gas mask', 'Children are safer in the country...leave them there'* and *'Put out waste bones – They make glue for aircraft'.* In addition to the numerous cap tallies, there were flashes, ribbons, badges, medals, battle flags and pennants of every description, plus swords, cutlasses, bayonets, daggers and knives. Even the Nazis were not left out, with armbands, leaflets, an *Achtung* plate and an Adolf Christmas card. Military memorabilia went on show with spurs from the Peninsular War, an Italian army bottle, officers' silver-capped canes and batons and, of course, portraits of Montgomery and Churchill. Other assorted items included castanets, a gold charger, the Admiral Fitzroy barometer, carved African figures, masks and bead necklaces, Dry Monopole jeroboams, a travelling beer barrel and, incongruously, a human and a monkey's skull. One amusing incident arising from the collection was when someone reported to the police that there was a bomb in the Fitzroy. Amid panic and consternation the Tavern was immediately evacuated, only to find that the deadly device was a Mills bomb in the collection. The detonator, of course, had long been removed!

Currencies from countries all over the world were thrown onto the ceiling. The Fitzroy was in fact 'invaded' every evening and became known as 'The Empire's Local', as 'all the year round visitors drop in there from all parts of the Dominions', according to *The Recorder.* The Tavern was known to every GI who came to the British Isles. As many American magazines wanted to know how London was coping, hordes of cameramen would swoop on the Fitzroy to photograph 'typical Londoners'. Among these were two celebrated photographers, Robert Capa and Karl Gullers. They took pictures in the Fitzroy which were seen throughout the world. Karl took a series of 150 photographs for a book called *England*, which depicted scenes and activities from every part of this 'scepter'd isle'. The English pub or local was of course portrayed by the Fitzroy Tavern. Robert Capa's photographs showed Annie pinning up badges and showing off her scrapbook of 1918 news cuttings. One personal bonus for Annie came from an article radioed to *Colliers* magazine by Walter Davenport, who had used her maiden name. When this article was published in Canada, Rosalie, the daughter of Pop's brother Oisia, read it and so managed to trace the family. Rosalie and Annie exchanged letters and Annie vowed if and when they ever retired she would like to take her family to the States and reunite the branches of the Kleinfeld clan. But retirement was a long way off yet!

Many of the Americans who frequented the Fitzroy in increasing numbers seemed remarkably uneducated about drink. They didn't appear to care what they consumed as long as it was alcoholic and had a kick in it. They had plenty of bucks in their pockets and were prepared to pay any price, unlike the hard-pressed Londoners struggling in times of rationing and austerity. One lunch-time a group of Americans ordered some drinks. That day, as was often the case in wartime, Annie was very low on supplies and was keeping back the small amount of beer for her regulars. She apologised to them and explained that she could only offer them some very old vintage brandy and at the exorbitant price of 7s 6d a nip. This was big money in those days, but the Americans were completely unabashed. 'Make them doubles!' was the response. Annie, realising the enormous profit on the sale, duly obliged, as she lined up the glasses on the counter, the American guy asked if she had any orange.

'Only squash,' said Annie.

'That's fine,' he replied. 'Pour some into the brandy.'

Appalled, Annie exclaimed, 'That's sacrilege,' took the brandy away and refused to serve them!

One American GI, Julius Horwitz, asked a policemen if there was anywhere in London like Greenwich Village, New York, and the bobby without any hesitation directed him to the

Fitzroy. He became so enchanted with the Tavern and Fitzrovia that, as soon as any leave was due to him, he was off there like a shot. He recalled these happy times with perceptive and empathetic insight and detailed observation in his novel published in 1964, *Can I Get There by Candlelight?* In a conversation with Denise Hooker quoted in her biography of Nina Hamnett, he captures the atmosphere of the war-torn city and the thrill at being in its throbbing heart.

> Coming into London, the blackout, bombs were falling, the ack-ack guns were out everywhere, those balloons were up with the wires...All you could think of was the immediate: how quick can I get to the Fitzroy, get a drink into me, a woman, who was Nina going to introduce me to, who am I going to meet. London became a great theatre.

Nina made a great impression on him and Nora, the central figure of his novel, is unmistakably Nina Hamnett. Dressed in shabby clothes, stockings holed or at half-mast, and down-at-heel shoes, she was nearly always drunk, dirty, picking up casual sailors on one-night stands and lacing her spicy anecdotes liberally with four-letter expletives. Too often Nina lay comatose in a pile of vomit outside the ladies' lavatory, though she did intersperse her binges with periods of feverish activity. She was disgusting at times, but also indomitable and endearing.

So Nina still kept a precarious hold on her Bohemian crown and was occasionally propped up by Augustus John. Ruthven Todd remembers the wobbly tripod of Augustus, Nina and Norman Douglas, arms linked and supporting each other as they weaved their way oblivious of the air raid above them and the nasty splinters of ack-ack shrapnel peppering the pavement. At least Nina remained in charge of the Fitzrovian intelligence service and, when a pub ran out of beer, she could pass the word quickly along the bush telegraph where more alcohol was to be had and the troops were realigned accordingly.

But at last peace came to war-weary Londoners and riotous celebrations were held all over London on VE Day and VJ Day. London was one big party and the six years of blackout disappeared in a blaze of light. The Fitzroy gradually returned to a semblance of normality and Charles realised that in the aftermath of the war the Tavern needed much repair and updating, particularly the cellars. The brewery agreed and, under the supervision of their chief architect Sidney Clarke, the latest Kelvinatore system of air-conditioning was installed, the first pub in London to have this. The beer could now be served at a constant cooled temperature, something the American customers loved, though the regulars were apprehensive at first. There was no need to 'fine down the beer' to settle it so it came up nice and clear, or to adjust the pressure system. All this was done automatically. The beer was filtered through transparent pipes from the barrels up to the bars, where it was dispensed through a pistol-shaped device. Annie liked the 'gun', but the idea never caught on. Annie hit the headlines as, 'ANNIE – THE PISTOL PACKING BARMAID', in true Annie Oakley style. As a result the cellars became the most up to date and cleanest in London. They were redecorated but not changed, in accordance with Pop Kleinfeld's farewell instructions to Charles and the brewers, Charringtons, 'You can build over my bars, under my bars, but *never* alter the insides.' Customers were invited to visit the cellars and cocktail parties were held there. They became Charles' pride and joy and looked more like a ship's spotless engine room than the cellars of a pub.

This new image of the postwar Fitzroy required a proper ladies' toilet. The loo was built on the ground floor between the two bars. While it was being constructed, Charles put a time capsule under the foundations which contained some coins of the day and some Fitzroy visiting-cards. This latest type of public toilet had a slot for the penny fitted to the door. Charles referred to these pennies as his 'bread and butter money'.

Though the pub was a tied house, occasionally they were allowed to break with this, as when the Fitzroy became the first London pub to sell Coca-Cola in bottles. This proved so successful that, when Charringtons decided to buy Canada Dry and introduce it into this country, they asked Charles to help them with their launch and promotion campaign. Charles made a most persuasive speech, which impressed the brewers and their chairman, Angus McKenzie-Charrington.

The end of the war had also seen a change in government. Clement Attlee's Labour Party swept into power and the Fitzroy became almost an unofficial headquarters and watering-hole for Labour politicians. Years before, the Tavern had been the venue for lunch-time debates. Hugh Gaitskell, Tom Driberg and Seymour Hicks would take the floor and students from the nearby London School of Economics flocked in to listen.

One day during the time of the Local Council elections a very angry group of students from the LSE stormed in. Annie had been campaigning for the local Conservatives and had smothered the bar with posters. Two women in the group started to tear these down, which made Pop furious. He went round to the front of the bar counter and in a loud voice said, 'How dare you take down those posters! You should know there is no such thing as politics in business!'

There was a deathly silence, but Annie, seeing the funny side of her father's remark, started to laugh. 'Dad,' she said, 'how can you make such a stupid statement when I put up the posters!'

This quickly diffused a nasty situation as everybody joined in the hilarity. From that day Annie became firm friends with one of the women, whose name was Dora Frost.

Dora returned Annie the favour when an anti-Semitic remark was made. She promptly picked up a pint of beer and threw it over the man's head. Hugh Gaitskell happened to be in the bar at the time and was immediately taken by this lady of spirit, and they struck up an acquaintance. Gaitskell was then a slim young lecturer and he was later to propose to Dora in the Fitzroy. When their engagement was announced in the Tavern, Charles slipped them a pound note so that they could celebrate in style. Leslie Hunter recounted this story in his book about the Labour Conference, *The Road to Brighton Pier*. Leslie was a regular Fitzrovian, attending what he called 'the world's most Bohemian pub'. He wrote *It's more than a pub, it's an institution* in a signed copy of his book which he brought in for Annie.

One day Annie received a phone call from Arthur Horner, the miners' leader, to say he was on his way to the Fitzroy with a crowd of delegates from the Trade Union Conference. Fortunately Charles was on hand, because instead of the expected pints of beer they ordered Pimm's. This was Charles' speciality. He professed to make the finest Pimm's in town and grew borage specially at his place in Somerset, while all through the war the Tavern was kept supplied with lemons by the sailors. Still, Pimm's for trade unionists was a surprise. What would Winston Churchill have made of it?

A whole host of socialist politicians and union officials patronised the Fitzroy, all throwing their contributions into the ceiling. Each year they sent Annie and Charles a card from the Labour Party Conference signed by them all – Aneurin Bevan, Herbert Morrison, Margaret Stewart, Barbara and Ted Castle, Michael Foot, Arthur Horner, Will Lawther and Ian Mackay. Ian was the acclaimed *News Chronicle* journalist who in 1949 described the Fitzroy as 'a place where always you will meet someone you know, Wilde and Whistler, Sickert and Epstein used it; Henry Moore and John still do'.

But the most loyal reporter of all was Tom Driberg. Tom had entered politics in 1942 when he was elected Independent Labour MP for Maldon, Essex. This was where in 1938 he had fallen in love with Bradwell Lodge – for many generations the Rectory House of Bradwell. Tom did not marry until he was forty-six, an event which quite astounded many of his close friends. Tom brought his wife, Ena Binfield, to the Fitzroy to meet Annie. Though Ena had Jewish parents, she became a Christian three months before she married Tom. The wedding was on 30th June 1951 at St Mary's Church near Sloan Square, and among the many distinguished guests were the Allchilds. Later on May Day 1953 he invited Annie and Charles to the launch of his new book, *The Best of Both Worlds*, at the House of Commons. He inscribed a copy for them, *To the Royal Family of Fitzrovia – in gratitude and affection.* But though Tom was always a stalwart Fitzrovian and friend, he was to cause Charles and one of the Fitzroy regulars, Albert Pierrepoint, some problems later.

The Fitzroy Tavern in the 1930s

Fitzroy Tavern visiting card

Judah Kleinfeld wearing the collar of the West London Hebrew and Benevolent Society

Judah behind the bar in the 1920s

The saloon bar with war posters

Father and son-in-law, Judah and Charlie, outside the Fitzroy

Annie and Charles Allchild

A group of Fitzrovians. Betty May is second from the left

Annie and her autograph book, open at the self-portrait of Augustus John

Albert and Annie Pierrepoint, Fabian of the Yard, Annie and Charles – a law and orderly quintet

Annie with Tom Driberg MP, the first William Hickey, who put Fitzrovia on the map

Card from Albert Pierrepoint's pub. Annie and Charles gave the former hangman advice on running the aptly named tavern

Annie adds a new cap tally to the collection

The Tavern adopted the crew of HMS *Fitzroy*. Although the ship was torpedoed, the crew survived to celebrate their rescue at the Fitzroy

Modern times...Annie demonstrates the beer gun

Nina Hamnett dedicated this 1931 photograph to Annie

A quarter of a century later, she made this brown pastel sketch of Sally

Sally launches her ship

A children's outing setting off from the Fitzroy, 1932

Betty May, Eddie Leech and Charlie with a group of children

Children's party at St. Pancras Town Hall. On the left of the platform is the cake weighing a quarter of a hundredweight. On the right is the 30 ft Christmas tree

Charlie and Annie and the Pennies From Heaven ceiling

The Crazy Gang collecting the paper darts of money

Richard Attenborough watches his wife, Sheila Sim,
throw the first dart towards the next party

Norman Wisdom and Annie Pierrepoint count the Pennies From Heaven

Lord Killanin, Michael Bentine and Ralph Reader help distribute food parcels

...and what better fun than a real clown you could touch

Alec Bedser presents Hercules bike to the lucky boy

Ralph Reader was in charge of entertainment at the parties...

Wynford Vaughan-Thomas (centre) gave a farewell speech to the Allchilds in
1956

The photograph of Dylan
Thomas which is displayed in
the Writers Bar of the Tavern

Sally with AJAX Sea Scouts

Sally names new ship Fitzroy

Mayor Harriet   Sally   Andre

Children from Fitzrovia Youth in
Action, with Sally, June Crown &
André Schott.

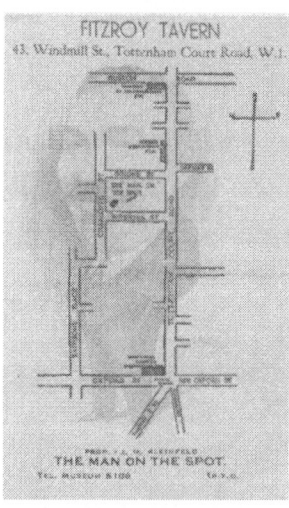

Pop's Original Visiting Card

Sally, Aeronwy Thomas & Clive Powell-Williams

Benny Green with Rickie Burman and Sally at the
launch of the Jewish West End project

Celine Hispiche as Betty May with Sally at the
1st development show of Betty May The Musical

Charlie – Arthur & Sally

5

Murder Most Foul

Undoubtedly there was a darker, more squalid side to Fitzrovia, a lurid underworld of crooks, black marketeers, prostitutes and pimps mingling in the pubs with regular customers and visitors. Aleister Crowley's satanic practices had shocked the public in the thirties, and in the same era the Fitzroy itself had provided the setting for an unpleasant murder.

One night Sylvia Gough turned up at the bar, badly beaten and sporting a black eye. Douglas Burton, a young writer, couldn't help noticing this. Burton managed to glean from the distressed Sylvia that her assailant had been another black magic devotee called Bose. According to Denise Hooker, Burton was an unbalanced individual, madly in love with the sensual Betty May. When the two men happened to meet at an artist's studio, in rage Burton struck Bose to death with the convenient weapon nearby – appropriately for Fitzrovia, a sculptor's hammer. After a trial which revealed the seamier depths of Bohemia, Burton was found guilty but insane.

This verdict saved Burton from the rope, which was the main working instrument of one of the Fitzroy's most unlikely customers, Albert Pierrepoint. Albert's career started when he was nominated as the Official Executioner like his father before him – quite a 'family business'. It ended in 1956, the year after he hanged Ruth Ellis, a *cause célébre*. Throughout this period he shunned any form of publicity for obvious reasons and it was only after the publication in 1974 of his autobiography *Executioner* that details of his life became generally known.

Despite his grisly job, Albert was a cheerful, unassuming man who struck up a great friendship with the Allchilds over the years. He would pop into the Fitzroy when he was in London, usually *en route* to the War Office before a 'professional' journey to Nuremberg. Albert was a small man who always wore a navy blue suit and dark tie and usually carried a raincoat and trilby hat. He never talked about his work except once when he explained to Charlie that his black case contained 'the tools of the trade'. These included the rope, the same one was used for all war criminals, but civilians were privileged to have a new one.

Albert adored children and, as he and his wife Annie had none of their own, he loved to go upstairs to the private sitting-room, put Sally on his knee and sing her nursery rhymes. When Albert and Annie decided to take over a public house in 1946, as novices in the trade they naturally turned to Annie and Charles for advice. Coincidentally neither of the two Annies drank alcohol and both were successful in running pubs. The inn, which was not far from where they lived, between Oldham and Manchester, bore the unusual name Help the Poor Struggler. In view of Albert's profession, this was quite a talking point and the press made cynical jokes about it, much to Albert's anger.

On one of his visits to the Fitzroy, Albert was introduced by Charles to a CID officer called Bob Fabian, later known as Fabian of the Yard, and they became firm friends. Then in 1947 a curious set of circumstances occurred which was to link them professionally. On 29th April 1947, everyone was shocked by the news of an armed robbery in Charlotte Street. The robbers had been disturbed and during their escape one of them shot and killed a man named Alec de Antiquis, who was trying to foil their getaway. The Fitzroy was picked as the murder headquarters and Bob Fabian was put in charge of the investigation. It was an exciting time, as Annie recalled, with CID officers meeting at the Tavern to discuss the latest developments. What they didn't know, however, was that Albert Pierrepoint had almost been an innocent witness to the murder. He wrote about the experience in his autobiography and later sent Charlie and Annie a hand-written letter describing what had happened, with permission to use the material in a book if they subsequently wished to. Albert also forwarded to them a signed copy of his own book, hoping that they liked it.

As it is really part of the Fitzroy story, here is Albert's personal account of the Antiquis murder:

In April 1947 I received a letter from the War Office asking if I was available to go down to London for an interview regarding a visit to Germany, which I accepted.

On my arrival in London I found I had a couple of hours to spare...so I decided to have a stroll down the West End, a place I loved to walk around and see how the other half live... It would be just after 2 p.m. when I was walking down Charlotte Street. I saw a crowd of people looking at someone on the floor. I looked at my watch and noticed that it was something past 2. My engagement was for 3 p.m. I thought someone had been knocked down so I pressed on to see...Charles and Annie Allchild...the Licensees of the Fitzroy Tavern, very close to where the crowds had gathered. I had a quick drink with Charlie and Annie, which they always brought me, then left for my appointment...

When I arrived at the War Office, I got my instructions for Germany and found they had booked me in at the Rubens Hotel at Victoria which was a transit hotel for officers – I had an honorary rank of Lt Col.

The following morning when I went down to breakfast I got the morning paper, and the headlines were 'Antiquis Murder in Charlotte Street'.

This came as a big shock to me, I don't know why, but I could not read any further than the headlines for quite a while. Then it hit me, that was the crowd I had seen the previous afternoon. I flew out to Germany that morning and a few days later I arrived back in London... When I phoned [Bob Fabian] I was told he was at the Fitzroy Tavern, a pub he was using as the HQ during the enquiries of the Antiquis Murder. Bob, although he never once asked me about my work, or vice-versa, did say a little about his case and I came to the conclusion he hadn't a clue at the time who he was looking for.

Charlie and Annie, being very good friends of Bob's and mine, always made us welcome, so we had a few drinks at lunch time at the Fitzroy Tavern and afterwards I left to catch my train home to Manchester.

A couple of weeks later I read in the press that three men had been arrested for the murder of Mr Alec de Antiquis, the father of six children. I then thought to myself 'Good old Bob, what a wonderful job you have done.' These three men were brought to trial and Jenkins and Geraghty were sentenced to death. The third man, Rolt, was sentenced to be detained during his Majesty's pleasure. On September 19th 1947 I was engaged to carry out their execution at HM Prison, Pentonville.

How ironic that their executioner only just missed seeing them commit the murder. The case itself, however, was to start much public uproar and controversy. Although Christopher Geraghty and Harry Jenkins were both sentenced to hang, it had been Geraghty who actually fired the fatal shot. Jenkins had been an accessory in the armed robbery. This increased public pressure for the abolition of the death penalty, as did the execution of Ruth Ellis. She was the last woman to be hanged, on 13th July 1955 at Holloway Prison. Pierrepoint was again the executioner. Ruth Ellis had shot her former lover, David Blakely, in a *crime passionnel* and had paid with her own life. As he told in his autobiography, Albert had been sent a cheque for ninety pounds as a bribe not to execute her, which cheque he kept, but of course didn't cash!

But there was a belated sting in the tale of the Ruth Ellis affair for Pierrepoint and Charlie. It all arose over an article Tom Driberg wrote in the *People* on 18th January 1970. The title was FOUR HOURS AFTER RUTH ELLIS WAS EXECTUED I SHOOK HANDS WITH HER HANGMAN. Tom Driberg had been reviewing the book *Women Who Murder*, and he described a purported meeting at the Fitzroy on the day of the execution with Charlie and Albert Pierrepoint; Tom was having a lunch-time drink in the Fitzroy and talking to Charlie, when the door opened and a powerfully built man walked in. He seemed to be a regular for he strode over to the bar and shook Charlie's hand. Then he shook Tom's. His hand was large and his grip was extraordinarily tight and strong. It was only then that Tom Driberg's memory clicked as Charlie introduced him. The newcomer was Pierrepoint the Hangman, and it was just four hours since those hands had adjusted the rope around the lily-white neck of Ruth Ellis.

As far as Albert was concerned, this was all a load of rubbish as he had never been over the steps of the Fitzroy that day, as he knew that the 'prowling press' would be about. Instead he went by police car to Bob Fabian's office and at 1 p.m. caught the train home, arriving very early. But he took particular exception to what Driberg said followed in the conversation. Charlie was meant to have asked Albert, 'How did it go?' to which Pierrepoint replied, 'Beautiful hanging, slipped away as smooth as anything.' Albert was so upset over this slur on his friend Charlie, who would never have asked such a stupid question. Professionally and morally Pierrepoint would never had made such a statement about the lowest person in the world, and to him Ruth Ellis was a 'heroine'. Pierrepoint therefore wrote to the editor of the *People* denying the article vehemently and demanding a written apology in the paper as it was defamation of character. All this was explained by Albert in a long letter penned in his neat, precise handwriting to Annie and Charlie dated 25th January 1970.

But Charlie and Annie were away at the time on a six-week cruise to South America and it was only their return in February that Charlie realised what had happened. He consulted his solicitor, but in the event Tom Driberg published an apology. This concluded, *although my account of the meeting as I recall it was given in good faith, I now unreservedly accept what Mr Pierrepoint says and am very sorry indeed for any distress which I have caused him.* After this public apology Charles, who had been great friends with both Tom and Albert, let the matter drop. Albert Pierrepoint throughout his career thought he was acting with dignity and humanity in carrying out executions as well as showing the utmost professionalism. But when he wrote his book he had changed his mind about the value of capital punishment. Perhaps as he approached the evening of his life he was trying to assuage a guilty conscience. Still, he of all people was best qualified to make such a judgment and his remarks are a salutary warning to the flog 'em and hang 'em brigade.

In the preface to his autobiography, *Executioner: Pierrepoint* Albert confessed:

> The fruit of my experience has this bitter after-taste: I operated on the behalf of the state what I am convinced was the most humane and the most dignified method of meting out death to a delinquent...[but] I do not believe now that any one of the hundreds of executions I carried out has in any way acted as a deterrent against further murder. Capital punishment in my view achieved nothing except revenge.

He went on to say in the last chapter:

> Executions solve nothing, and are only an antiquated relic of a primitive desire for revenge which takes the easy way and hands over the responsibility for revenge to other people... If death were a deterrent, I might be expected to know. It is I who faced them last... All the men and women who I have faced at that final moment convince me that in what I have done I have not prevented a single murder.

Albert's friend Bob Fabian was not the only detective at the Fitzroy Tavern. Jack Capstick, Fred Narborough and Jack Rutherford were also customers. They were respected not only by the Allchilds but by the criminals themselves. Annie remembered one day when a man pushed his way through a crowd of people at the bar, went up to Bob, warmly shook his hand and offered him a drink.

'Who was that?' Annie asked him.

'Oh, a man who I put inside and has just come out,' came the answer.

But not as friendly was the chance meeting between Wally Thompson, ex-robber, and Jack Rutherford, ex-CID, who had helped to start Scotland Yard's Flying Squad. Jack had been employed as a potman-cum-overseer and minder for the Fitzroy after his retirement from the force. At first the encounter was frosty. After all, Rutherford had arrested Thompson twice and on a third occasion had brought him in for questioning at gunpoint. There was a thirty-year feud between them which went beyond the hatred of crook for copper. This really was a *High Noon* confrontation, charged with tension. At first Rutherford didn't notice Thompson as he was bending forward to pick up glasses.

'What's the matter, Jack? Don't you talk to your old friends now?'

Rutherford spun round and stared at Wally. 'I always speak to my friends,' he said. The voice was cold and sarcastic. Then Rutherford walked down the bar, his hands full of glasses. He was still a great bulldog of a man, thick-necked with bulging biceps.

But Wally wasn't going to let him escape that easily. Raising his voice above the hubbub, he shouted, 'Old Jack was a terror in the force. But I got my own back. Remember the time in that pub when I pinned the paper to the back of your coat, Jack?'

The buzz of conversation around suddenly ceased as customers were gripped by the face-off.

'I remember it all right,' Rutherford snapped with venom. 'You set it alight and then and the boys squirted me with soda siphons to put the fire out.'

The atmosphere was now electric as the vicious repartee continued. 'Got me after that. Nicked me for a load of watches and clocks from a jewellers.'

Rutherford laughed unpleasantly. 'That's right. You got four years.'

'But what Jack didn't know,' quipped Thompson, 'was that when he picked me up the woman I was with had a £1,000 worth of jewels in her purse. And she got away.' Wally smiled smugly.

Not to be outdone, Rutherford reminded Wally, 'Remember at the Angel, I was chasing you when you ran into a blind alley. You ducked into a house but couldn't get the front door shut.'

'And I stuck my hand in my pocket,' said Thompson, 'and made out I had a gun. I made you stand there while I backed away.' Wally paused dramatically and with superb comic timing added, 'And then two uniformed coppers grabbed me from behind!'

At this point both laughed. The ice was broken.

'Life's a lot quieter now,' said Rutherford.

'For me too,' agreed Wally.

'Drop in for a drink some time.'

'I'll do that.'

The feud was over and everyone resumed their conversation. The cushioning of the years and the relaxed atmosphere of the Tavern had done the healing job. But this was typical of the Fitzrovian magic.

6

Pennies From Heaven

That special magic of the Fitzroy Tavern was nowhere better displayed than its famous 'Pennies From Heaven'. The ceiling money idea had originated in the early twenties with darts filled with money thrown onto the ceiling. This brainchild of Pop's at first was called 'The Fitzroy Money-Box' but soon acquired the name 'Pennies From Heaven' – after the song made famous by Bing Crosby. The customers were thrilled with this novelty, which soon caught on. Up to this time the Tavern had arranged many Christmas parties for the old folk at the Drill Hall in Chenies Street, but now Annie and Pop wanted to do something different with this ceiling money which was growing quickly. The first time it was taken down in 1923 it amounted to thirty pounds, in those days a large sum of money!

Jane and Pop adored kids and in the twenties there were many poor and ragged children in London. Annie suggested that they might like a day in the country as thirty pounds would be enough to take a hundred children on a country outing. Annie and Pop found a few willing helpers and asked customers to select likely children and muster them outside the Fitzroy at 8.45 a.m. They were then marched crocodile fashion down to Great Portland Street Station. The ticket-collector on counting heads discovered there were 134 children but Pop couldn't turn them away and immediately busied himself getting more food and presents. So off they went to this idyllic place just outside London called Eastcote! Over the next couple of years the amount of money swelled and by 1930 the amount off the ceiling had risen to £87 6s 6¾d. Gradually the number of children increased to five hundred. This was far too many to go by train and a very generous customer donated thirty pounds to hire ten charabancs.

Annie was an excellent organiser. She encouraged many of the famous customers to act as helpers, such as Betty May, Gwyn Evans and even Desio Vaiani. Norah James gave the prizes, while others took on the role of honorary secretary and games officer. Gwyn Evans in particular delighted the children by dressing up in various costumes. She insisted right from the start that the children chosen could be of any race, creed or colour. Fitzrovians were given application forms to fill in stating name, age, sex, address, who had recommended them and who was the parent or guardian of the child. Annie also issued coloured tickets that had to be tied onto each child. She even applied to Tottenham Court Road Police Station to see if the police could close Windmill Street to traffic while the children were departing and arriving back after their day out. Not only did they agree for the first time to close a London street for such an occasion, but they also arranged for all the traffic lights to be on green. This ensured the long convoy of coaches of children, dignitaries, stewards, helpers and St John's Ambulance members could stay together. Each child was given a bag containing fruit, sweets, crisps and drink for the outward journey, and amidst resounding cheers the Mayor of St Pancras waved them off on their fantastic day out. They would sometimes go to Chipperfield Common, Boxmoor or Brickets Wood.

When they arrived the children lined up to receive from Pop Kleinfeld a new shilling to buy gifts. The St John's Ambulance Brigade pitched their tents in case of emergency then the stewards divided the children into age groups to take part in games and sports like egg and spoon, sack and three-legged races. There were donkey rides and merry-go-rounds, and it wasn't just the children who had a fabulous time. They all tucked into a bumper tea afterwards. Annie and her parents used to marvel how the kiddies devoured the goodies. It was a real joy. All the way home the children sang and cheered; there to meet the happy band all carrying their prizes, gifts and bunches of bluebells at the Fitzroy were their parents and guardians.

In those early halcyon days it was very much down to Annie, Pop and Jane, plus the helpers, but after the war new personalities came onto the scene to administer and organise the fund-raising and parties for children. The first of these was the ebullient Ralph Reader, famous for his wartime Gang Shows and post-war annual Scout Gang Shows. Ralph loved coming to the Fitzroy, which he used to say was 'a colony not a pub, where the great and near-great and down-and-outs were citizens lorded over by the Governor and his lady with a membership stretching to the ends of the earth'. He regarded Annie and Charles as:

> Two very dear Jewish people who stand out in my life and because of them I could go into battle when fools deride the Jewish race as a whole.

Ralph was the obvious choice for Honorary Director of Entertainments on the committee they now decided to form. After the war it was no longer practicable or appreciated by children to hold the outings again. Most of the children had been evacuated to the country during the war and by now the ceiling money had multiplied exceedingly. Plans were under way to take down all this money from the ceiling and start something new for London's orphaned and poor children. The idea was to organise and hold each year a gigantic New Year's party for 504 deserving children.

To join Ralph, Annie and Charles approached Lord Killanin. The Rt Hon. Michael Morris, 3rd Baron Killanin, had been a regular at the Fitzroy since the early thirties when he was an undergraduate at Cambridge. It was Wynyard Browne, the playwright who wrote *The Holly and the Ivy*, a contemporary of Lord Killanin at Cambridge, who first introduced him to the pleasures of the Fitzroy, although in fact he had known Judah Kleinfeld even before the Fitzroy days when he went to have his Eton suit fitted by the Savile Row tailors where Pop was working. A fine sportsman, he started as a journalist and had a distinguished war record in the King's Royal Rifle Corps, taking part in the Normandy landings and rising to the rank of brigade major in the 30th Armoured Brigade. In 1945 he married Sheila Mary Dunlop, who had worked as a decoder for the Foreign Office at Bletchley Park in the war and received an M.B.E. for her efforts. They returned to Ireland to his family home at

Spiddal, Co. Galway. Sheila was also Irish, and Michael said he had married 'the local parson's daughter'. Subsequently he was associated with films, and became President of the International Olympic Committee. Michael was the ideal person to be Patron, but at first was reluctant. As a peer of the Irish realm, he didn't have a seat in the Lords, so did Annie really want him? But he had a high regard for his Jewish friends, the Allchilds, and applauded their charitable enterprise. Annie in her indomitable way won him round. 'Michael, the Cohens and the Kellys have always got on well together!' she said. After reconsideration Lord and Lady Killanin readily agreed to perform this prestigious role, which they fulfilled with distinction over the years.

The last two people to join the committee were the local police sergeant Arthur Hanson as Honorary Secretary (his wife Joyce had often helped Annie in the bars during the war), and a customer, Miss Tiddy, who consented to be Assistant Secretary. The main organising and planning was still Annie's job but Charles was now able to see that everything was done with military precision.

People from all walks of life, trades and professions came not only to drink but to throw their contributions onto the ceiling, while schools phoned to bring parties of children to see the ever growing collection of war memorabilia. Charles had by now perfected his system for the paper darts to a fine art. He would come round to the front of the bar with the red, white and blue paper ready prepared. Meticulously he used to extract the small cork washers from the tops of beer bottles and place these in the centre of the paper. A tack was then inserted through the middle when the customer put the money into the paper. Charles screwed it up tight to form the familiar dart shape. 'Drum roll!' he would shout to the resident pianist, Reg. 'Right, Guv,' Reg shouted back, and he would strum out grandly and with theatrical flourish a succession of chords. This announced to all that another packet of money was to be thrown into the ceiling. Charles would first demonstrate how it was done.

Probably the most famous celebrity to take part was Ingrid Bergman. When she came one night, it caused quite a stir. Ingrid refused Charles' offer of the paper and instead took out of her handbag a blue handkerchief. 'Why not?' thought Charles to himself, and took her hankie, placed a cork in the centre and put a tack straight through it. Ingrid placed her thirty shillings in coins into the handkerchief and after Charles had fashioned it into a dart, threw it onto the ceiling, where it stick – to an enormous cheer from all present. Everybody naturally wanted to have a go and get a dart as close to hers as possible, and this brought in a lot of money.

Before the first party could be held, the money had to come down from the ceiling. Annie and Charles decided that this would make a unique occasion to gain publicity. They applied for a special after-hours licence and invited personally some of the generous Fitzrovians and press to a special Pennies From Heaven champagne party. This was their way of saying thank you to their benefactors. There was one practical problem. The money on the ceiling was from many countries and much of it was now out of circulation. Annie went to her local bank, the Midland in Tottenham Court Road, which in the past had helped her so often. She told them of her difficulty, the manager 'listened' and the bank agreed to honour any currency taken down from the ceiling. So on Wednesday 29th December 1948 the first Pennies From Heaven party was held. The ceremony was broadcast on the *In Britain Now* programme of the BBC Overseas Service with the commentary by Wynford Vaughan-Thomas. For the event the heavy steel tables were lined up along one side of the saloon bar and large square biscuit tins labelled to show the different currencies placed in a row across them. At one end was put the latest type of adding machine, kindly lent by the National Cash Register company. Starting with the bank manager, a rota of people totted up the money.

Wynford never forgot that night, describing it as his 'shakiest assignment'! Charles, 'assisted' by the Crazy Gang and Jack Hilton the band leader, was the first to take down the money. Charles had made a special double-sided ladder as the ceiling was extra high. Wynford, microphone in hand, mounted the ladder, perched himself on top and calmly started to describe the ceremony to the listeners. What he didn't realise was that Jimmy Nervo and Teddy Knox had gone up after him. They lifted his trousers, rolled down his socks and proceeded to tickle his legs while he was giving his commentary. Wynford, not surprisingly, found it difficult to maintain his balance and composure, but in true broadcasting tradition somehow managed to continue. The show must go on!

Everyone joined in the party spirit, helped by a liberal supply of champagne. Adelaide Hall wrote in the visitors' book, *They only give you champagne here!* As every hundred pounds was recorded on the adding machine a huge cheer went up. All the Fitzrovians who had thrown their contributions onto the ceiling took their turn to pluck it off. It was a glittering celebrity showcase. Among the cavalcade of stars were Arthur Askey, Eric Portman, Beverley Nichols, Louis Golding, Kingsley Martin, Barbara Castle, Michael Foot, Hugh Gaitskell, Bob Fabian, Albert Pierrepoint, Arthur Wragg (the jockey), Murray (the escapologist), Norman Parkinson, and Lord and Lady Killanin. This was the one time that singing was allowed in the bar. The law at the time permitted music – hence the piano – but no singing or dancing. But this was a private affair, and the film star Dolores Gray climbed the ladder to sing most appropriately *Pennies From Heaven.*

The partygoers were quite a mix. Angus McKenzie-Charrington was naturally invited, but one surprise guest was Geoffrey Bing, QC, MP, the Socialist member for Hornchurch. At that moment he was not at all popular with the breweries as he was trying to introduce a bill to nationalise them. In fact he gained the nickname of 'Bing the Bung'. To overcome any embarrassment, Annie decided the best thing was to introduce the two gentlemen to each other. Despite everything they got on very well in the festive atmosphere.

At last all the money was taken down and sorted. There was every currency under the sun from dollars, yen, Hungarian forints, pesos, kroners, Siamese satangs and even pounds, shillings and pence! When the final total for the night was calculated, the Mayor of St Pancras, Councillor Lillian Bryant, declared it to be £575. All were delighted and there was still the foreign currency to be added to this. Charles then invited Richard Attenborough and his wife Sheila Sim to throw up the first packets of money to start next year's collection. Sheila bent down and scooped up Raffles, the Tavern's perky Pekinese puppy, while Charles handed the money-filled dart to Richard to launch the missile to the ceiling. The successful landing of this lonely packet was soon followed by a serious of similar packages in the next hour.

This first year did have its own particular problem. After the party, the money was taken to the bank. The dust and dirt which had accumulated over the years was dreadful and the money was so filthy and almost unidentifiable that the bank couldn't accept it. Then the manager came up with an ingenious suggestion. Why not take it to their Billingsgate branch as they had the facilities for washing money and putting it back into circulation? This they did and all was well. Gifts and donations flooded into the Fitzroy from all parts of the world. It was rather like the modern Children in Need and Telethon appeals. There were food parcels from the Hoyts Theatre Group in Australia, Sunkist oranges from California and sweets, chewing-gum and signed photos from the stars in Hollywood. These included Xavier Cugats, Charlie Chaplin, Shirley Temple, Bob Hope, Walt Disney (signed by Mickey Mouse), Joan Crawford, Roy Rogers and Dale Evans. When the boxes of chewing-gum arrived, Sally knew they would please the children. She had never seen so many varieties, most of which had not been heard of in England before.

As the news spread far and wide so did the customers' support for the unusual way of collecting the money. Other stage, radio and television stars became interested in the scheme – Trevor Howard, Ava Gardner, Dickie Henderson, Bebe and Ben Lyons. The former Vice-President of America, Henry Wallace, threw up an autographed dollar bill. Tommy Cooper, Richard 'Stinker' Murdoch and Kenneth Horne often came in for a drink and would project their change onto the ceiling. Kenneth Horne was a particularly generous person and helped get Sally into his old boarding-school, St George's, Harpenden. Tommy Cooper was also great fun off and on stage. He was only worried during the months his wife was expecting, as he confided to Annie over his pint. When Thomas John was born, Annie sent Gwen a flower arrangement in the shape of a fez.

But the Pennies From Heaven parties were only the precursor of the children's parties, which were to be held for the next nine years and became renowned as one of the annual events of London. The first of these children's parties took place on Sunday, 3rd January 1949 at the Assembly Rooms of St Pancras Town Hall. The preparation had been going on for months. Arthur Stannard, a Fitzrovian whose brother owned a printing business, donated the most incredible number of essential items – application forms, letterheads and different-coloured tickets to indicate the different ages of the children, which ranged from six to twelve. Annie had to fill all these in as the Commercial Union had donated a million pounds' insurance cover. Then there were the instructions for the various categories of stewards and helpers, the invitations for guests, table plans and even special carrier bags for the children to take home their gifts and goodies after the party.

Only helpers and children were allowed into the Assembly Rooms. Specially invited guests were seated in the balcony, where different arrangements were made for them. Arthur knew that, in spite of his generous contribution, he didn't fit into these categories. He was determined though not to miss out and the only way was to dress up as a clown. The children loved him in this role.

The kiddies picked for these parties were mainly groups. Annie particularly remembered the Vicar, Rev. Jimmy Dumfries, who each year brought a group from his church, St Philip's in the Old Kent Road, and also Rev. Alexander Amias, the Cantor from the West End Great Synagogue in Soho. These two reverend gentlemen as specially invited guests sat in the balcony. Despite their different religious faiths, they great appreciated each other. The Vicar put his hat on and the Cantor took his off as marks of mutual respect. This afforded Annie much pleasure as one of her aims was to bring the people together.

Annie, despite this, was always aware of her Jewish faith and had insisted that the party be a 'New Year's party' to be always held on the first Sunday of the year. She could not bring herself to think of it as a Christmas party, but really this was its theme. Therefore, as Charles pointed out, the party needed a

Christmas tree. Charles wrote to Fred Peart, the Minister of Agriculture, to see if they could have a tree like the magnificent one given by the people of Norway and erected in Trafalgar Square. Fred Peart replied that, though there were difficulties, they were not insurmountable. Jack Shearn, who owned a fruit and flower shop in Tottenham Court Road, was in the bar that day and he offered to pay for a tree. After that, every year a thirty- to forty-foot tree, supplied by the Forestry Commission, was driven through the streets of London with a large placard *This is for the Fitzroy Tavern's New Year's Party.* It would then be put up by the Town Hall staff, decked with hundreds of special lights and topped with a beautiful fairy, a three-foot walkie-talkie doll which was to be the prize for the lucky youngest girl.

The parties were simply fabulous. The Assembly Rooms had been transformed into a Christmas Wonderland. At the first party there were forty-two tables set with places for twelve children. That is why the number of children invited to these parties had to be precisely 504. On each table was a show card with a pantomime title – *Mother Goose, Sinbad the Sailor, Jack and the Beanstalk* etc – so the children would know where to sit. Every year the theme was changed. Once it was famous sportsmen – Gordon Richards, Steve Donoghue, Roger Bannister, Jack Hobbs, Jimmy Greaves. These were all hand-painted by one of the Australian customers, Miss Betty Richie.

Annually a souvenir brochure and menu was produced. Particularly memorable was the first, by the Fleet Street columnist Ian Mackay. He entitled it *The Good Fairy Pop* and wrote that 'it did not matter if the children were Christian, Jew or Arab or Black, White or Yellow, if you were a child recommended by one of the customers of the Fitzroy as one of London's needy children you were welcome to the party. All you had to do to make Pop love you was to be a child!' Other Fitzrovians were to reveal their versions of this unique story in the forewords – Stanley Jackson (the journalist), Louis Golding, Beverley Nichols, Frank Owen (of the *Express*), Gale Pedrick (author and producer) and Wynford Vaughan-Thomas.

The party started and the excitement mounted as the Mayor and Mayoress, Annie, Charles and Ralph Reader appeared on the stage to a loud fanfare of music from The Modernaires. Charles gave the children a rousing welcome and the Mayor read out a message from HRH Princess Elizabeth and the Duke of Edinburgh. Also revealed in full splendour was a quarter-cwt cake donated by a local baker which a Fitzrovian like Eric Portman or Marilyn Hightowers was going to cut with a sword taken from the bar and carefully cleaned by Charlie.

The only time the guests from the balcony could come down into the hall was while the children demolished the tea. Often the children didn't know who these 'special' people were. But they all recognised Leslie Compton, the Arsenal footballer, who brought every year a football signed by the team as a prize. Of course they knew the Mayor because he was dressed in his regalia, complete with chain of office. There was one other gentleman they loved. He was always laughing and joking with them. They called him 'Uncle Albert'. The next morning in the *St Pancras Journal* the headline read HANGMAN BRINGS LIFE TO A PARTY.

Next on the party agenda a Fitzrovian in the disguise of Father Christmas delighted the children. Each year a different personality was selected. The first was Bruce Belfrage, and he was succeeded by Ian Mackay, Richard Dimbleby and Stubby Kaye. The Sea Scouts had constructed a sleigh for Father Christmas to be brought onto the stage. In 1955 it was quite different though. The world was full of excitement at the first launching of a Sputnik so the Sea Scouts in their effort to be up to date made the most incredible rocket as the transport for Father Christmas. It was Gilbert Harding who, with great sportsmanship, experienced the joys of space travel. Santa would hand out presents to all the children – comics, chewing-gum, sweets and signed photos of the film stars, even a real Sunkist orange (most had never seen one as they had only drunk the Government orange juice during the war), a gift from the California Fruit Growers Exchange. The kids received an extra thrill as BOAC, who shipped the oranges over, brought a stewardess in full uniform onto the stage. There were gasps all round from the children as this was their first glimpse of an air hostess.

Ralph Reader was in his element at the parties. He brought together a host of stars of stage, screen, radio and circus to provide great entertainment for the children. Unbelievably Michael Bentine was so shy of performing in front of such a young audience that he had to be pushed onto the stage! Charlie Drake, Dickie Henderson, Norman Wisdom, Carole Carr and Coco the Clown, plus some of Ralph's own Gang Show 'boys' and not forgetting Shaggy the Dog, took part. The customers had made Shaggy a magnificent coat in gold and green with his name on it. He did his act on stage with Charles playing football with balloons. Annie was never sure who enjoyed it more, Shaggy, Charlie or the children!

The final part of the afternoon was the much awaited announcement of the raffle prizes. Annie was overwhelmed by people's generosity. Ralph always made a feature of the presentation and the lucky winners were invited onto the stage where Annie, who was to present the prizes, Charles and many of the performers stood to receive the children and wait with them until it was their turn. The top prize in Annie's eyes was a bicycle donated by Hercules Bicycle Co. Ralph used to get the children to say after him, 'I wish it was me...but I'm glad it was you.' The first year the oldest boy won the bike.

'Sonny, have you got a bike?' Ralph said to him.

'Oh no!' he gasped. 'I've always wanted one.'

Annie said she really had to control herself to stop the tears flowing.

There were many other great prizes. One was for a boy or girl to be completely fitted out with clothes. Annie arranged a time with the parents after the party and together with Arthur Hanson and any brothers or sisters they all went to Dawson Bros in City Road. They were clad from top to toe, from underwear to topcoats, and then taken to Lyons Corner House for tea. A few shillings' change always remained for pocket money shared between all the children.

The climax and finale of the party came when the youngest little girl received the fairy doll from the top of the Christmas tree. At Ralph's signal the lights of the Assembly Rooms were dimmed and a spotlight fixed on the doll. As if by magic the fairy flew from the top of the tree right to the happy little girl. It was a very moving and impressive moment as everyone cheered. What no one could see was the *deus ex machina*, Charlie behind the tree manoeuvring the elaborate pulley system he had rigged to get the doll down. After all this fun and excitement the children went home tired but happy, each clutching their Fitzroy bag filled with presents and goodies.

Some years were particularly memorable. In 1949 Derek Rock, the actor who played 'Just William', did a special sketch written by Richmal Crompton, and Terry Thomas also entertained the kids. In 1950 the children at the local University College Hospital who could not attend were not forgotten. A delicious tea party was held in the children's ward and a television was presented. By 1951 the parties had become such a London institution that BBC Children's TV televised it live. The programme was meant to be for one hour, but overran by twenty minutes.

Charles himself was no stranger to TV shows and broadcasts. One such broadcast went out to every English-speaking country in the world, entitled *The Britain That Nobody Knows*. A few days later he was invited by Gilbert Harding to be a guest on his TV programme *The Spice of Life*. As Gilbert had been a loyal Fitzrovian for many years, Charles readily agreed, although it meant that for the first time in all those years he would be away from the Fitzroy on a Saturday night. This was his opportunity to pay tribute to Gilbert, who, as he described on the show, was 'one of the kindest men I have ever met'. The programme was a great success and Charlie even managed to get back to the Fitzroy before closing, in time to answer viewers' messages of congratulations on the way he had honoured Gilbert.

But the most ambitious undertaking of all took place in Coronation Year, 1953. Charles and Annie wanted to commemorate this historic time in a unique way. They also desired to thank Ralph Reader for his unstinting work as Honorary Director of Entertainments – but how? After a discussion, Ralph said he would be over the moon if the Tavern could buy a boat for the 4th Surbiton Ajax Sea Scouts. He had learnt that an ex-naval pinnace was for sale at £600. Without hesitation Charles and Annie said, 'Buy her. Tell us what else she wants and we will see what we can do.' The ship was moored on the Medway near Maidstone, Kent, and the troop leader, Chiefy Sharman, went down to inspect her. The craft was fifty foot long from stem to stern and required a complete overhaul. Chiefy, with some of the scouts, sailed it up the River Thames to their moorings at Kingston. The scouts were all thrilled at having their own training ship.

But it was an enormous task to convert the boat into a ship suitable for training scouts, and they sought expert advice. Chiefy came into the Fitzroy a few weeks later, bubbling over with excitement. If the ship was to be recognised by the Admiralty, she needed a lot of equipment. He was almost too scared to tell Charlie, but he gave him the list. Charles was unruffled. He presented the 'little list' to customers and had an immediate response. Pye Radios gave a ship-to-shore radio, Piggot Bros international flags, Joe Coral the bookmakers galley equipment, Beverley Nichols and Louis Golding a ship's library, John Line paint and varnish, Uttoxeter Potteries china, Charrington's Brewery ship's fenders and the National Cash Register Co. cash. Gilbert Harding didn't want to be left out.

'What's left?' he asked.

'A hundred feet of sisal rope,' said Charles.

'Put that down to me.'

Uncle Dick also wanted to contribute and paid for the ship's bell.

After the ship was towed to dry land, repairs to the hull were carried out and she was completely repainted. The troop's parents formed an association to raise funds too. At last the day came when Chiefy announced that she was finished. For her to be recognised by the Admiralty only one more thing remained – the ship had to officially named and the Scouts wanted Sally to do it. This called for a celebration. On the morning of Sunday, 19th July 1953, the Allchilds were up early. Charles had made a cradle for Chiefy to fix on the ship's bow, and a bottle of champagne was placed in it for the naming ceremony. Invitations had been sent to all Fitzrovians who had contributed so generously, parents, press, scouts and, of course, Ralph Reader. The crowd excitedly waited at the troop's moorings at Surbiton for the ship's arrival. A euphoric cry went up as the little fleet was sighted. Whalers, dinghies and rowing-boats were led proudly by the Training Ship *Fitzroy*, dressed overall with her flags of international code. The whole troop, immaculate in uniform, stood to attention on the deck. The local vicar gave his blessing, and prayers were said for the ship and crew. Then came Sally's big moment. Chiefy handed her an enormous and very heavy 'train tapper's' hammer. As she crashed the bottle of champagne, she proclaimed, 'I name this ship Training Ship *Fitzroy*. May God bless her and all who sail in her.' There is a Jewish saying, 'One *quells* (gains) much *nachas* (satisfaction) from one's children.' It was not just Sally's big occasion that gave Annie and Charles such tremendous satisfaction but the pleasure it gave the Scouts, who they looked on very much as 'their boys'. The ship now officially named by Sally, TS *Fitzroy*, was duly acknowledged by the Admiralty and later by the Ministry of Defence. This meant that Scouts who trained on the TS *Fitzroy* and entered the navy would probably get a commission. Lord and Lady Baden-Powell agreed to become joint patrons of the Fitzroy Tavern Children's Pennies From Heaven fund, as the Allchilds had done so much for Scouting over the years. Annie had become Vice-President of the 2nd Oxhey Scouts Troop and Charles had received the Bronze Wolf Badge.

Neither were the customers overlooked at this Coronation time. Charles had found a glass goblet with the royal cipher, on which the name of *The Fitzroy Tavern* could be etched on the foot. Annie agreed this would be a fitting souvenir of the Coronation to give their customers, and Charles went ahead with an order for hundreds. The glasses were not just to be presented to Fitzrovians who came into the Tavern, but were also to be sent to nearly every country in the world. When the first assignment arrived, he set to experimenting how he was going to package the glasses.

'There's only one way to try and see if they survive,' he said to Annie. 'Go outside and stand on the opposite side of Windmill Street.'

'What?' asked Annie.

He repeated himself and added, 'If there's anyone in the bar, tell them to go with you.'

Mystified, she did as she was told. Charles took three packages and ran up to the top floor of the building and out of the hatch onto the roof.

'Annie,' he shouted, 'is it clear below?'

'Yes,' she called back.

'Stand clear and watch,' Charles warned, and a couple of seconds later three small packages wrapped in brown paper were flying through the air from the Tavern roof before landing on the road.

'Everything all right?' he asked.

'Yes,' replied Annie, still baffled.

'Pick them up and meet me in the bar.'

When they all gathered in the saloon bar, Charles explained that he was testing the strength of the glasses. 'If they survive, we're in business.' They removed the wrappings and all the glasses were perfect. They were overjoyed and the customers in the bar became the first of thousands of Fitzrovians to receive these much treasured souvenirs of the Queen's Coronation.

Another interesting year was 1955, when the Pennies From Heaven party was something else! Remo Bertorelli, one of the sons, had taken over the family business and now specialised in ice-cream and frozen confectionery. He asked Charlie and Annie if he could use the occasion to promote his new ideas. 'You won't be sorry,' he promised.

In spite of it being a cold January day, the atmosphere was glowing with anticipation. Tommy Cooper went up to what he thought was a hot-dog stall. It was actually the Bertorelli barrow, complete with monkey. Barbara Castle handed him what seemed to be a sausage and egg. In fact it was ice-cream. Indeed all the food was made of ice-cream. Out of jars marked mustard came spoonfuls of zabaglione, the salt was sugar, pepper ground nuts, vinegar a liqueur and so on. The supreme dish created for the function was called Cassata Fitzrovian. It was not until 3 a.m. that the real secret of what the sausages and eggs were made of was revealed by 'Gellato Charlee'. The sausages were honey-nut ice-cream shaded brown and the eggs were contrived from praline-coated ice-cream and zabaglione. Julie Adams said that she had never tasted or been to anything like this before, even in America! It was all great fun and an enormous success, with nearly £700 raised that night towards the party.

7

The Battle of The Fitzroy

But the happiness of 1955 was marred by a dramatic event which had a most unpleasant sequel. It was 9.50 p.m. on 15th January, a busy Saturday night at the Fitzroy. The pub was heaving and Charles was busy pulling pints for customers who were thronging the saloon bar three deep. His attention was caught by a gentleman in plain clothes who came round the side door to speak to him. Charles felt slightly uneasy and asked him what was his business.

To his shock, the stranger replied, 'Observation has been kept on these premises on the 7th, 8th, 13th and 14th January and during this evening, sir. The officers have seen many perverts who frequent this bar behaving in a disgusting and disorderly manner. They have also seen drunkenness here. My officers will take the names of all present with a view to possible proceedings.'

Charles and Annie, who had now joined her husband, were dumbfounded. Annie pulled herself together sufficiently to ask the man where he was from.

'I'm Superintendent Paull from Tottenham Court Road Police Station.' Charles quickly added that of course they would give the police every facility and assistance.

The police started taking names and addresses, and to Charles' mortification they arrested two women customers for being drunk. One was Stella Wearmouth, a thirty-year-old married woman who was sitting against a table singing. The police described her speech as thick and slurred and that when asked to get up, she was unsteady on her feet and upset some beer. Mrs Wearmouth indignantly denied that she was drunk – only merry. She had consumed six half-pints of light ale – her usual quota at the Fitzroy. Later she was accused of being a convicted prostitute but Charles had always found her well-behaved and smartly dressed and she often came in to the Tavern with a young man, whom he took to be her fiancé.

The other lady, Margaret Garner, was much older – eighty, in fact. Mrs Garner had been sitting in the corner drinking what the police took to be stout. Actually it was Guinness, and according to another customer she had drunk two of these and a large tonic – without any gin. She also suffered badly from arthritis and Charles explained she had difficulty in walking. But the police reckoned she had staggered across the bar to the ladies' lavatory nearby and on her return had nearly fallen down. She kept saying the same line of a song, 'You can't trust the specials like the old-time coppers'. Perhaps these words incensed the police. Yet unfortunately for Charles and the two ladies concerned, Dr James Gossip, who examined them at Tottenham Court Road Police Station at 11 p.m. that evening, formed the opinion that they were both drunk.

Charles and Annie were shell-shocked by the police raid, but Charlie did have the presence of mind to intervene and calm down a potentially explosive situation. Soon after Superintendent Paull entered, a scuffle broke out between a marine and a sailor. They were parted by Charles, showing great firmness. When the police finally left, Charles and his wife considered the implications. They had received no warnings of any kind from the police before the raid that something was wrong at the Tavern. Naturally, the clientele of the Fitzroy included people from all walks of life and the sexual preferences of customers were irrelevant to Charles and Annie. Later Tom Driberg, Beverley Nichols and Rupert Croft-Cooke were to admit publicly their homosexuality. What of it? To the Allchilds they were always charming, personal friends, faithful Fitzrovians and great supporters of their charities.

It was hard in the bar crush to keep track of undesirables causing disturbance, and Annie, her father and now Charles had done all they could to keep up the pub standards. Still, Charles and Annie took the Superintendent's advice and consulted their solicitor W. Timothy Donovan. Even so, they had an interminably long time to wait before the summonses were served and they knew exactly what the charges were and on what dates the offences were meant to have occurred. The legal delays were very worrying for Annie and Charles as their recollection naturally was fading in the interval. Eventually the summonses arrived in May but it was not until 21st June 1955 that the case finally came up before the Magistrates' Court at Marlborough Street. The summonses were in three batches. The first charged Annie and Charles with being the keepers of a house where intoxicating liquors were sold and knowing and permitting disorderly conduct therein. The second was for permitting drunkenness under S.136 of the Licensing Act (1953) on 7th, 8th and 15th January in the Tavern. Finally there were two summonses for selling intoxicating liquors to drunken women, Stella Wearmouth and Margaret Garner, on 15th January.

This *cause célébre* or, as Charles preferred to call it, 'The Battle of the Fitzroy', The Police *v.* Charles and Annie Allchild, was heard by the magistrate, Paul Bennett, Esq., V.C., MC. Mr R. E. Seaton was instructed by the Solicitor to the Metropolitan Police to appear for the prosecution and Mr Donovan instructed Mr G. D. Roberts, Q.C. and Mr Gilbert Rountree for the defence. Hartley Shawcross had initially been briefed, but he had to decline from pressure of work. Still, the legal luminaries arrayed for the defence were formidable adversaries for Mr Seaton.

'Khaki' Roberts began the trial with a 'most emphatic' plea of Not Guilty to every summons. Battle was well and truly joined as Annie and Charles were determined to vindicate in every possible way the good name of the Fitzroy.

There followed some legal skirmishing by the alert Mr Roberts. First, the prosecution were trying to include prostitutes as well as homosexuals before 15th January under the omnibus umbrella or *ejusdem generis* rule of disorderly conduct. As the magistrate himself commented, is soliciting disorderly if a lady whispers to a prospective client? Secondly, the long delay had been most unhelpful to the defence. Finally, as the Superintendent was in court while the first police witness was being examined, the magistrate agreed that Superintendent Paull be politely asked to leave.

95

But these were all relatively minor preliminaries to the full frontal assault by Mr Seaton in his opening address. In a hushed courtroom he made the accusation that the Fitzroy was a 'den of vice'. Charles turned to Annie in disbelief. The reporters present with pens poised started scribbling frantically as Mr Seaton detailed his charge. This emotive phrase was taken up as headlines by the *Daily Mirror* and *Daily Express* the next day but the prosecution argued that the lurid epithet was in no way exaggerated. A large number of people in the bar on the nights of 7th, 8th, 13th, 14th and 15th January were 'homosexuals' who paraded themselves unashamedly as such. They blatantly had dyed hair, rouged cheeks and behaved effeminately, speaking in high voices. These 'perverts', they alleged, were attempting to seduce members of Her Majesty's Armed Forces – sailors, soldiers and marines – in a most disgusting manner. According to the police, it seemed as if the 'homosexuals' were overrunning the place. They had made a head count of up to 60 'perverts' on the seventh, 70 to 75 on the eighth, 50 to 55 on the thirteenth, 60 on the fourteenth and 80 on the fifteenth. What detailed observation and analysis by the police!

The 'perverted behaviour' had apparently involved fingering sailors' buttocks, linking arms with sailors, rubbing their thighs and generally kissing and patting each other on the cheek. Shock, horror – they had even put hands up a Seaforth Highlander's kilt! At such an outrage the motto *Nemo me impune lacessit* sounds a hollow boast. According to Mr Seaton, these 'perverted homosexuals' accompanied the brave servicemen down to the gents. The conscientious policemen followed them downstairs to the lavatory, where they saw two 'perverts' and two sailors standing close together and one of the sailors was buttoning up his flies. What in incriminating action after urinating!

The language allegedly used was indeed colourful. They addressed each other as Diane, Sylvia, Monica, June and Georgina respectively. One typical comment was, 'I can't stay all night,' the 'lady' is meant to have said, 'Don't worry, my dear. I shall look after you.' Again Georgina supposedly told her friends, 'It was awful... He turned out to be a bloody old steamer. Two pounds for all night.' 'I bet you told him what he could do with it,' Sylvia answered to gales of laughter. Another rich interchange reported by the police ran as follows:

'Excuse us, we are going down the hole,' said the sailor.

'If you are going to wash your hairbrush, can we come and dry it for you?' the 'pervert' responded.

'I don't get it but I'm willing to learn,' the bewildered sailor said.

This brought titters from the packed courtroom.

A further sample was, 'I think you are two lovely boys. You must both come home with me when we leave here.'

Even more extreme, according to the police, was when one 'lady' stood on one leg on the bench seat, exclaiming, 'Here I am Cupid, God of Love,' and was complimented on a 'nice round bottom'. The police would testify that during their periods of observation sailors trooped off with 'homosexuals' for assignations together outside the pub. All this time neither Mr Allchild nor Mr Rutherford, his trouble-shooter, appeared to take any notice of the 'outrageously lewd behaviour' and comments. They could quite easily have both seen and heard all this although they were busy working and the noise in the bar was deafening.

From Mr Seaton's onslaught, the Fitzroy seemed to Daniel Farson like a Port Said brothel with sailors on a spree going wild with houris and transvestites. To add further spice to this scenario, prostitutes were seen soliciting on the premises. Two ladies of the street mentioned were O'Hara and Whatton. On 13th January the diligent PC Pyle saw O'Hara approach a middle-aged man by the bar, smile and accost him, 'Hello darling – on your own?' When he replied he was just there for a drink, she went on, 'Would you like to come with me for a short time when you have had your drink?' The policeman observed them leaving the bar soon after. Just as quickly she returned, and with the other prostitute Whatton later went out, each with a man they had successfully propositioned. The next day PC Pyle again noticed the pair in the bar talking briefly to potential customers, and Whatton even had the temerity to approach the police constable himself. 'Are you looking for a naughty girl or a naughty boy?' she said as she smiled winsomely at him. Not surprisingly he replied, 'Neither,' and refused her offer of a trip home. Undaunted, PC Pyle on the fifteenth heard the persistent Whatton asking a man behind him if he was alone and was interested in fun with her.

This then was the general thrust of the prosecution attack which Mr Roberts and his defence team had to rebut. 'Khaki' marshalled his forces skilfully. He argued most persuasively that with the noise and chatter in the crowded bar, the piano playing and the tills clanging, it would have been very difficult for the landlord, Jack Rutherford or any bar staff to hear any conversations of prostitutes and 'homosexuals'. It was all they could do to take drink orders, serve the customers and sort out the change. The police were also challenged about O'Hara and Whatton being convicted prostitutes. There was no proof and no records were available to the court. Whatton had in fact been in Birmingham on 7th January, the night in question. To complicate matters further, after their period of observation at the Fitzroy the police 'snoopers' had moved on the Marquis of Granby to watch the goings on there. This had inevitably resulted in confusion of identity and evidence in their note-taking between what they saw at the two pubs. Significant delays in the note-taking seriously reduced their value, according to Mr Roberts, and therefore the whole prosecution case.

However, the defence counsel's main target for cross-examination was the mastermind and initiator of the raid on the Fitzroy, Superintendent Paull. The Superintendent admitted that the covert spying operations had taken place on his instructions without any prior warning, and this despite good relations in the past and a commendation by the police. He had only been at Tottenham Court Road Police Station since the previous May, and the suggestion was that he had acted for self-aggrandisement in the force. His entry to the pub that night had brought not peace but a sword as the raid had provoked the scuffle quickly settled by Charles Allchild. Under cross-examination he was forced to agree how difficult it was for a licensee or a member of the bar staff to decide if the man he was about to serve was a 'pervert'. A high-pitched voice and a gentle, even effeminate manner didn't necessarily mark out a person as such.

But the corner-stone of the defence case was Charles Allchild himself. Charles was determined to give a good account of himself and the Tavern. When he stepped into the witness-box, he was first asked about any police commendations. Without hesitation he replied:

'Well, it was with reference to a woman who was wanted by the police in various parts of the country. We understand she had been drugging men and robbing them. She was known as "Dopey Dora" and there had been much talk and publicity about her.

'Eventually this woman came into the Fitzroy one lunch-time. We had never seen her before in our lives. She opened a conversation with me with reference to the ceiling.'

In fairness, Mr Roberts at this point interrupted Charlie's evidence. 'I think you need not go into too much detail, because it is not strictly relevant.'

But the learned magistrate wanted to hear out the story and overruled him, commenting, 'It is very interesting. You had never seen her before?'

'Never,' said Charles. 'The woman came into the bar and said she had travelled all over the world and had heard about our wonderful ceiling collection. (She was obviously after the money.) I thanked her very much. We gave her the usual paper, she put a donation in it and it went on the ceiling. A few minutes later Mrs Allchild came into the bar and said, "This lady had given her name as –" and I forget for the moment what it was. There was a CID chief inspector of Tottenham Court Road in the bar. Mrs Allchild went over and had a word with him and she said, "I do not like this woman. She is worthwhile checking up on." I kept up a conversation with this lady –'

The magistrate then butted in, 'To cut a long story short, was she arrested?'

'Yes,' said Charles, 'and got seven years.'

'Did she really?' said the magistrate and he stroked his chin reflectively.

How ironic that teamwork between the police at Tottenham Court Road and the Allchilds had produced a conviction and commendation, and now the same police station under a different regime without a friendly word of warning had launched a raid on the Tavern. As Charles explained, the previous Superintendent, Mr Munday, had made himself known to them on several occasions. Charles had always been strict regarding potential troublemakers. Any doubtful character was first kept under observation by the ex-CID man Rutherford before being asked to leave. It was Charles' proud claim that no one had ever been accused of soliciting in the Tavern until the present unpleasantness.

Charles Allchild also disputed the police testimony regarding the night of 7th January. They had said that Charles wasn't in the bar that evening, but Sally had written in her diary that her dad had cut his finger that night. It all came flooding back to Charlie. He had indeed cut his thumb very badly when opening a beer bottle just after 9 p.m. and had tried in vain to stanch the bleeding – blood splattered the counter, pewter and floor. A customer, Mr Fletcher, volunteered to take him to the nearby Middlesex Hospital to get the wound dressed, and off they went. Further inconsistencies in the police evidence came to light when they said that on 8th January Annie Allchild was not present in the bar. In fact Sally was given a chocolate box on that date by a customer, Mrs Hawkins, at 9.30 p.m. and Annie received it for her. These errors in the police evidence affected the whole credibility of the prosecution.

Both customers and staff refused to believe what the police had professed in court. Many wrote letters of support and others gave evidence on the stand. Wynford Vaughan-Thomas, then employed as a BBC broadcaster, said that he used to go there twice a month and had never seen anything revolting or disgusting. People of both sexes frequented the bar and he and his wife Charlotte were of the opinion that 'the house was always conducted in an orderly manner'. Other married couples called said they liked the homely atmosphere of the Fitzroy and would certainly not have gone there if it was a 'den of vice'. These included Mr Putt who had served twenty-eight years with the Met, Geoffrey Bing, QC, Mr Davey, a local government officer, Mr Brodsky, a journalist, Mr Stanfield, a retired teacher and Mrs Clifton, a housewife. Others such as Fred Narborough and Bob

Fabian all agreed to be called as character witnesses, but in fact did not give evidence.

Out of the actual pub staff, the most important witness was undoubtedly John Rutherford, the overseer. He categorically declared on oath that he 'had never seen large numbers of perverts in the house and although the place was usually crowded the customers were well-behaved'. It was, of course, in his interest to say this as it was his responsibility to eject undesirables. Even so, he was quite specific about the procedure to be followed in case of potential trouble. If anyone was not up to scratch he would be politely told to leave and wouldn't be served. If there was misbehaviour, the culprit would have to leave immediately. When a problem arose, communication was by nod of the head without the customer knowing. The code word was 'Margate'. This gave him a single ticket and no return.

Supporting testimony came from Henry Amos Bruce, known to everyone as Harry, who had been working as a pot/bar man at the Fitzroy for twenty-six years. He was virtually a fixture there. Also Charles Tipper, head barman with just over seven years' service at the Tavern, gave evidence, as did Reg the pianist, or to be precise Reginald Stanley, who had tinkled the ivories from 7 or 7.30 p.m. to closing time every evening. The other barmen, Mr Finn and Mr Carlisle, gave evidence too. None had seen disorderly conduct, and the gist of their combined evidence was that they could not hear and see much when they were so busy serving.

In his concluding speech for the defence, 'Khaki' Roberts pointed out that the defendants were of the highest integrity with a clean slate as far as the police were concerned and even commendations. The case was not one which gave the police any cause for pride. Superintendent Paull, a newcomer to the area, had set in motion a prying operation with no warning to the licensee, as if he was operating in a police state. Unfairly, the days selected for this surveillance were Fridays and Saturdays, when the pub would be most over-crowded between nine and nine-thirty. The saloon bar was a comparatively small room, and with the piano playing, the din of conversation, five cash registers ringing and banging, and the laughter and merriment, how could a busy barman serving half a dozen customers at the same time hear what one homosexual was saying to another in the corner? For that matter, how could the snooping policemen hear as well? In the same way, Charles Allchild could not have seen a 'pervert' fingering a sailor's buttocks lasciviously when he was serving them drinks. As they were facing him on the other side of the bar counter, he couldn't see through the counter and the men's bodies. It was just like Sam Weller, who without a pair of double million magnifying glasses had limited 'wision' which couldn't penetrate a deal staircase and a pair of deal doors. Clearly the prosecution evidence was grossly exaggerated in depicting the Fitzroy as a 'den of vice'. Instead it was a decent house run by eminently respectable people.

But for all Mr Robert's eloquence, on 30th November the complex trial ended with the summonses against Annie absolutely dismissed while Charles was convicted on nine of the counts and fined £1 on each. The magistrate dismissed the police claim for costs of 75 guineas and £4 10s expenses because of the long delay involved and the resultant heavy financial burden on the defendants. Mr Roberts immediately announced his client's decision to appeal against the conviction. Charles was in the depths of despair and his customers were equally aghast.

James Norbury summed up the feelings of everybody in his letter to Charrington on 1st December 1955. He admitted that 'the pub [had] a certain Rabelaisian flavour [but] so [had] the Cock Tavern in Shakespeare's day and so [had] the Café Royal in the 90's. After all if a pub has to have the smugness of a primitive Methodist day out, it ceases to be a place of good fellowship and this loses its significance and purpose'. After listening to the evidence he felt the police had overstated their case with a 'series of very carefully devised half-truths, in some places, and deliberately calculated lies in others'. He feared we were 'deteriorating into a police state that could only have found its parallel in Nazi Germany or Fascist Italy'. James was even more eloquent with righteous indignation and exclaimed, 'Has the day come when a man goes to a respectable public house to be spied on without his knowledge or when the landlord and his wife, who have been known for many years for the care with which they manage their house can be used as a catspaw for a police supervision and raid without being given any warning of any kind? Alas, our boasted English freedom is slipping very badly if these conditions are allowed to continue...where the landlord and his wife are innocent parties of police persecution...'

James happened to be in the Fitzroy himself some ten minutes before the raid took place on 15th January and categorically denied that any of the conditions were true at the time he was there. How in that short space of time could a place that hummed with good fellowship turn into what the police described as a den of iniquity and depravity. To provide further rebuttal of the police claims, James was in the Tavern when one of the incidents described by the police took place. His own version runs thus.

'A crowd of young soldiers, obviously out for a night's spree, were drinking merrily at one side of the bar, a piano broke out in lively tune and a couple of the soldiers in question broke into a semblance of a tap dance. It was obvious they were not drunk, it was clearly obvious they were not annoying anyone and Mr Allchild took steps immediately to quiet them down, but then this seemed quite unnecessary in the jovial atmosphere of the pub that evening. This simple incident, young servicemen getting rid of their exuberance and energy over a pint of beer and a merry tune, might have been indulging in an orgy of drunkenness if the police description of this incident is correct.'

This account by James Norbury is admittedly and avowedly partial but serves as a corrective to the licentious picture painted by the police.

Further support for Charlie was given by Vivian Cox in a letter to the brewery in which he described the Allchilds as 'presiding genii' of a 'house we have come to love and an atmosphere so wonderfully preserved amid the crumbling relics of a vanishing Bohemia'. Another well-wisher was Sir Charles Irving, who immediately sent an encouraging telegram from Cheltenham: NO COURT OF LAW COULD CHANGE MY VIEWS OF ONE OF THE BEST COUPLES WHO HAVE DONE SO MUCH GOOD. SUCCESS AND GOOD LUCK WITH YOUR APPEAL. IF I CAN DO ANYTHING I SHOULD BE ONLY TOO HAPPY. DON'T WORRY. IN THE

MINDS OF THE MAJORITY YOUR NAMES ARE CLEAR AND YOUR HOUSE IS JUST AS ALWAYS PERFECT. SINCEREST GOOD WISHES.

But despite this stalwart Fitzrovian support this was the most awful worrying time pending the hearing of the appeal, particularly as Sally was critically ill. Every customer would ask how Sally was and one sailor, Carl Hayman, got the whole of his ship's company to pray for her return to health. Neither the near-miss bombing nor the trial had shaken Charles and Annie as much as Sally's condition. But at least she was in good hands at University College Hospital.

At last the waiting was over. The appeal lasted two days, starting Wednesday 11th January 1956. Then just as it was getting under way Annie and Charles received a catastrophic letter from Charrington out of the blue. They had decided to suspend Charles until the appeal result and he was given notice to quit the Fitzroy. It was a real bombshell and they were devastated. The case had not been concluded and they had such a record of success and enjoyed such prestige through the trade and the world. Did this really mean nothing at all to the brewers? The customers were in uproar at this shabby and high-handed treatment.

But from the gloom of their despond they were overjoyed by the verdict of the London Sessions Appeals Committee, chaired by Frank Cassels. Charles was acquitted on all charges and the £9 fine imposed by the magistrate lifted. The great news spread fast and the London evening papers had the reports. The headlines proclaimed the successful verdict – BAR LICENSEES WIN APPEAL (*Star*), APPEAL SUCCEEDS (*Evening Standard)* and THE FITZROY COUPLE CLEARED (*Evening News*).

When the delighted Charles returned from the court to the Fitzroy, the first thing he did was to dash up onto the roof of the Tavern. Flushed with the effort and triumph, he patriotically hoisted the Union Jack. His belief in British justice was vindicated and the good name of the Fitzroy was cleared. The customers ecstatically welcomed their conquering hero back. Yet though the main 'Battle of the Fitzroy' was over, there was still a rearguard action to be fought. 'We are not out of the wood yet,' he told the packed Tavern that evening, when drinks were on the house. 'We look like making licensing history because I don't agree with the notice to quit which is due to expire at the end of the month.' Charles was in fighting mood as to cheers from his Fitzrovian cohorts he announced, 'I am prepared to ignore the order, even to the extent of physical eviction.' The drinking was long and deep that night.

The next morning, as Charles cleared his head, he was cheered by the avalanche of telegrams and letters of congratulations. Sylvia Gough sent, 'congratulations and love', while Rudolph Dunbar wrote rejoicing in the appeal verdict which had 'rectified a gross miscarriage of justice'. The national papers all covered the story. CLEARED LANDLORD FIGHTS FOR PUB, said the *Daily Express*, and the *Daily Telegraph, Daily Herald, Morning Advertiser, Reynolds News, St Pancras Chronicle, Marylebone Mercury* and *North London Press* gave full reports.

The brewers were astonished at the result and the reactions of the customers. Charringtons had been bombarded with the most amazing letters of support for Annie and Charles. Now Sir Edward Chadwyck-Healey, Charrington's chairman, decided to make the directors review their decision. They belatedly begged the Allchilds to stay. But the toll had been enormous; it had cost Charles thousands to clear his name and that of the Fitzroy. Even more, they felt they had been let down and devastated by the brewers. Most unpleasant of all, Charles had received poison-pen letters from someone who had it in for him. One of these vitriolic and salacious epistles contained a crude drawing and mentioned 'disgusting goings-on in the lav', and the author threatened to write to Sir Edward Chadwyck-Healey about it all. The other referred to a soldier and 'homosexual' kissing each other in the lavatory. It ended ominously, *Beware Allchild. I'm watching you.* Needless to say, no names were given and the writers' identities were never discovered.

So though the battle was finally won, Charles and Annie had gone through enough. They had made the Fitzroy into the 'Rendezvous of the World' as it had been called. Annie and Charles were proud of their achievement. And now in the elation of victory, yet soured by their treatment at the hands of

Charrington, they decided to call it a day and announce last orders.

8

Last Orders

Charles' resolve to call it a day and retire marked the end of an era. Charles was adamant about his decision. To Annie the thought of leaving the Fitzroy was dreadful, but deep down she knew that Charles was right. They needed a break, Sally was still weak after her months of illness, and as Charles used to say, 'All good things must come to an end.' With their triumph in 'The Battle of the Fitzroy' and the vindication of their good name, Charles and Annie were leaving at the top with their heads held high. It could never be the same again. The scene and the people had changed for ever.

In the first place, Pop Kleinfeld, the founder of the Fitzroy, had died in May 1947. The *Morning Advertiser* on Saturday, 10th May 1947 announced POP OF THE FITZROY IS DEAD...AND THE WORLD MOURNS. Judah was called, 'the Santa Claus of Soho', the Fairy Godmother to many, a man who was justly proud he had no enemy anywhere in the world. Hundreds attended his funeral in Streatham, where he was laid to rest beside his beloved Jane. The most poignant moment of all was when Charles threw four pennies into the grave – the four pennies that Judah had had when he first came to London all those years ago. So that his contribution to the licensing trade might never be forgotten, Annie sent a hundred guineas to the Licensed Victuallers School in Slough to be used as a Memorial Prize For Dramatic Work and Verse Speaking.

Indeed, Judah Kleinfeld had played an immense part in the pub trade. He had changed the Fitzroy from being a derelict public house stuck away in a corner on the edge of Bloomsbury to a meeting-place for artists, writers, public figures and celebrities from every walk of life. Slowly, with the infinite patience of a coral building up the beauties of the Great Barrier reef, Judah Kleinfeld turned the Tavern into a personality and ensured the Fitzroy was a place of good fellowship, kindness and humanity.

His customers too had passed on. In 1953 Wynford Vaughan-Thomas came in to the bar looking very distressed. He told Annie that he had just heard the terrible news of Dylan Thomas' death. Wynford had known him since their schooldays together in Swansea. Alcohol had clouded his later years and on that final lecture tour in America he had not gone 'gentle into that good night'. Annie remembered the days when she had thrown him out of the Fitzroy. But in spite of his drinking problems he remained a brilliant poet and writer. Annie readily agreed to Wynford's strange request, 'Would you allow me to hold a memorial service to Dylan in the bar tonight?' That evening a most moving short service took place in the saloon bar of the Fitzroy conducted by Wynford Vaughan-Thomas in honour of the immortal bard from Laugharne. As soon as the ceremony was over, Wynford passed his hat round and the donations were then thrown on the ceiling.

Alcohol also speeded the end of perhaps the most loyal devotee of the Fitzroy, Nina Hamnett. Over the years her drinking had become even heavier. Long-standing friends like James Norbury and E. J. Moeran still kept in touch with her after she moved to the Paddington area. She returned to the Fitzroy for fitful excessive drinking sessions. After one heavy binge in May 1953 she was so inebriated that Annie ordered her a taxi home. A few days later Annie learned that she was in hospital with a fractured thigh-bone. Nina's time at Paddington General Hospital turned out to be like a holiday, with good food and comfort which she had not experienced in years. When she was discharged she seemed to have a new lease of life and would often be seen in the saloon bar of the Fitzroy working on the second volume of her autobiography *Is She a Lady?* 'I'll have a gin, m'dear,' she would say if anyone had the temerity to interrupt her concentrated efforts. 'Make it a double!'

She still retained her liking for rough-and-tumbles with young sailors, but her mobility was seriously impaired after she returned to hospital in August 1954 to have the pin removed from her leg. One leg was now shorter than the other and she could only limp gamely about with the aid of a stick and built-up shoe. Her visits to the Fitzroy became sporadic and she would be visited by friends in her squalid rooms in Westbourne Terrace. Yet she could rouse herself from her despond, as when publishers seemed to be vying with each other over her new book. In February Nina sent a card to Annie on which she scribbled, *Publishers rushing for my book. Victor Gollancz just too late alas. I have sold it to Alan Wingate for £100 and royalties and they hope serial rights. Wild excitement all round. They think I will make £1000 this time. Serve them all right doesn't it again after twenty years. I think this one is much better ha ha!* But Nina's euphoric optimism was misplaced and short-lived. *Is She a Lady?* was a disorganised hotchpotch and inferior to her first volume, *Laughing Torso*.

Unfortunately by now Nina's chronic alcoholism had affected her nervous system and her hand shook so much she could hardly hold a brush. She became very depressed and thought she had contracted VD. The final straw came when she felt she had been savagely caricatured in Bob Pocock's radio play *It's Long Past the Time.* At lunch-time on Thursday, 13th December 1956 Nina fell forty feet from her window and was impaled on the railings below. She was rushed to Paddington General Hospital and given an immediate blood transfusion but to no avail. Her faithful friend James Norbury wrote in detail to Annie and Charles about her last days:

'Now about darling Nina. I wrote to her...asking her to let me know if she would like us to pick her up in the car on Saturday morning and take her out to lunch. On the Wednesday of that week Bob Pocock's programme on Charlotte Street in the Thirties had been on the Third Programme and Gladys Young gave a magnificent impersonation of Nina in those days. Your father was mentioned of course and many of the folks we all knew and loved in those good old days, gone now never to return.

'Well I had no reply from Nina but the following Monday received a very abusive letter, most unlike her, called Bob Pocock all the names she could think of and saying we had all deserted her. Well, as I had gone to see her regularly this sounded very odd so I wrote back and told her I would go and see her the following Saturday.

'On the following Thursday evening I was just having a bath when the phone went. Bryan answered it and said you are wanted very urgently, it is about Nina. I slipped on a bath robe, rushed to the phone to find it was Paddington Police Station to tell me that Nina had had an accident, had fallen out of the window and was in a very serious condition in Paddington Hospital. A few minutes later Eileen Coyle, very much the worse for whisky, rang and said, "You must meet me at once, Nina has committed suicide."

'I rang the hospital, spoke to the sister and she told me Nina was in a coma but in no immediate danger and I arranged to go round later that evening. I then rushed down to town to meet Eileen, drunker than ever this time, and telling all and sundry that Nina had committed suicide, that she had tried to gas herself twice and cut her throat once before throwing herself out of the window. Luckily at that moment Bob Pocock who I had phoned and asked to meet me turned up and off we went to the hospital. I saw the sister who asked me if I knew the address of any of Nina's relatives. The only one I knew was Viva King in Thurloe Sq. so I contacted her and she said she would let the relatives know that Nina was in a very dangerous condition. I stayed at the hospital until the early hours of the morning then went home leaving my phone number as they said they would call me if there was a change for the worse. On the Friday morning they operated for internal injuries and on Friday evening they let me see Nina for a few minutes but she looked terrible. I had a quiet word with the doctor who told me there was no hope at all but she might linger for a week or two. On Sunday afternoon I had just had lunch when the phone went and the hospital said could I get over at once as Nina was dying. I rushed into my coat, Bryan got the car out and at that moment the phone rang again. It was the hospital to tell me that Nina had just died. It was exactly twenty minutes to four.

'...On Monday I received a phone call from the Coroner's Office asking me if I would go to the inquest on Tuesday morning to give evidence of what I thought from my long knowledge of her, of Nina's state of mind. He then mentioned Eileen Coyle and all the rumours. I saw the danger light as we didn't want a suicide verdict, and told the officer that Coyle was a typical Soho type, more often drunk than sober and always full of idle and malicious gossip. "So you don't think she could help us if we called her?" I told him I didn't and she wasn't called.

'In the meantime Nina's local doctor had been in touch with the police and told them that he thought she was a very unstable character so they decided to call him to the inquest. Then the fun really started. The hospital doctors were charming. One mentioned to me the gash in the throat but said that as she died as a direct result of the fall they didn't intend to mention this at all. The inquest went off very well until her local doctor got into the box. It was his big moment and he was determined to make the headlines and the nasty swine did.

'The point at issue was that some weeks previously Nina got it firmly fixed in her head that she had got VD. Well, years ago when she had contracted it she went to St Thomas's Hospital for treatment so off to St Thomas's Nina went once more for a blood test. The test showed all clear and we all thought the incident was closed. Not at all. The local doctor in the witness box said that he had heard that his patient unknown to him and without consulting him in any way had been to St Thomas's for certain tests for a certain disease. The coroner, bless his heart, tried to shut him up, but on and on he went and at last the coroner said, "Well I am going to adjourn the inquest until tomorrow morning while I make routine enquiries from St Thomas's although I feel it is quite irrelevant to the matter we are discussing." He then agreed that we could proceed with arrangements for the funeral and cremation and the next morning brought in a verdict of accidental death. Well, the funeral was ghastly. Nina would have laughed her head off had she been there. The relatives decided that if in life she had been a Bohemian of the first order in death she must be a Christian and they had the lot. A lot of old friends turned up and that was that.

'...Well that is the full story. The press were wonderful and of course all discovered what a magnificent artiste Nina was once she was dead.'

Annie and Charles were so sad to receive James' tragic tidings about their friend. At least the coroner, Mr Bentley Purchase, had given Nina the benefit of the doubt though rumours inevitably continued. After her cremation at Golders Green Cemetery, some of her friends gathered for a wake at the Fitzroy and toasted Nina as they had done Dylan Thomas a few years earlier.

But even though so many old faces had gone and life at the Fitzroy could never be the same again, it was still a great wrench for Annie to leave the Fitzroy. After all, she had started it with her father. In particular she would miss the children's parties. At least she had given the children a farewell party to remember. This thirty-third and last children's party was the biggest that Annie and Charles had ever organised. It was held on Sunday, 1st January 1956 at a different venue, the Scala Theatre, Charlotte Street, so that 700 children could attend.

Each of the children received paper hats, novelties and a tuck box full of goodies to eat, as well as toys, games, books and comics. As a small reminder of the day everybody present was given a brand-new penny to keep for luck. Ralph Reader excelled himself with the show, which featured top acts of the day. The kids were entertained by Coco the Clown, the juggler Jose Moreno, Sylvia and her amazing Chimpanzee, Frances Keep, Britain's No. 1 Punch and Judy Show, The Merry Martins stars from pantomime at the Golders Green Hippodrome, and Mick and Montmorency involving the irrepressible Charlie Drake. The wide-eyed children were amazed when for the finale the Band of the Grenadier Guards in full uniform marched and counter-marched and played for the audience. This was the first time the band had played for a non-military and non-ceremonial event. The Guards joined with the Scouts Band, and as the music reached a crescendo, Ralph led everybody in community singing, ending inevitably with *Pennies From Heaven, The Crest of the Wave, We'll Meet Again* and the National Anthem. The three cheers that followed for Annie and Charlie nearly raised the roof! Annie said, 'If we ever do this again we'll need the Albert Hall.'

Not to be outdone, the last night at the Fitzroy saw the final Pennies From Heaven party. Annie and Charles threw the most extravagant champagne party for all Fitzrovians and the press. It was broadcast by the BBC, with Wynford Vaughan-Thomas doing the commentary as usual. Among the many guest celebrities were Vera Lynn, the outgoing Forces Sweetheart, and Petula Clark, the incoming one. These and Fitzrovian faithfuls over the years all took their turn to mount the double-sided ladder to pluck down some of the money. Adelaide Hall invited everyone to join her in singing *Pennies From Heaven* as Charles held up a huge board with the words displayed. Fitzrovians numbered Leslie Compton, Tony Mercer, Barbara and Ted Castle, John Arlott, Kenneth Horne, Richard Murdoch, Tom and Ena Driberg, Norman Wisdom, Louis Golding, Gilbert Harding, Richard Dimbleby, Gale Pedrick, Sheila and Michael Killanin, Hugh David, Herbert Morrison, Vivian Brodsky, Beverley Nichols, Norah James, Rupert Croft-Cooke, James Norbury, John Pudney, Rudolph Dunbar, Noel Johnson, Richard Attenborough and Sheila Sim, Yvonne de Carlo and many more. There were a lot of Fleet Street journalists from the *Standard,* the *Express, Morning Advertiser* and *Television Newsreel,* as well as policemen Jack Capstick and Bob Fabian with their respective wives, Albert and Anne Pierrepoint, lawyers Judge Frank Cassels and Geoffrey Bing, besides local businessmen, representatives from Charrington, including their conscientious Area Manager Harold Knee and Angus McKenzie-Charrington, many of the crew of HMS *Fitzroy* and family members too. It was a tremendous gathering; the champagne flowed and the atmosphere was phenomenal, even though this last party was tinged with an air of sadness that the Fitzroy would never be the same again.

As the guests milled around them, Annie said, 'It isn't our Fitzroy. The staff are a little mellow, they all feel sad. So do we, but...' She shrugged her shoulders.

Charles leaned across. 'Now we shall have a rest. We've earned it. We'll not come back into the trade, but we'll miss it.'

As Bernard Levin wrote in an article for the *Manchester Guardian* on 27th March 1956, it was 'the end of a chapter at the Fitzroy, the Tavern where Arts and Politics mingle.'

The party concluded with a wonderful toast to the Fitzroy and its hosts by their loyal friend, Wynford Vaughan-Thomas:

'For thirty-seven years this ship has chartered the seven seas; to the furthest corners of the earth without sailing one knot. Just over one year today she ran into troubled waters – pirates boarded her in an endeavour to scuttle and sink her. Our Captain and his mate Ann piped battle stations; and for one whole worrying and nerve-racking year, they battled against overwhelming odds, and even at the times when all seemed lost they refused to pipe "Abandon Ship".

'Today with all flags flying they brought the ship unstained, safely to port where she is securely moored.

'Ladies and gentlemen, I ask you to be upstanding and drink a toast to our skipper and his mate!'

Annie and Charles had deserved this accolade.

So the pub was stripped of its valuable wall collection, including the full-size oil painting of Judah by one of the customers, the Countess Anna Monici. The precious cloak of dust that had settled on the posters over the years was carefully gathered and packed by Charles and handed out as souvenirs! 'Give me some of that,' said a young man from Quantas Airlines. 'I'll sprinkle it over Australia.' Off came the gimmicks – pennants, cap tallies, drums, spears, swords and swordfish. The next day the pub pianist Reg played *We'll Meet Again* but with a difference. As his fingers glided over the keys, the piano was lifted and so was the stool and both were pushed outside the Tavern. The removal men then hoisted the furniture of the new licensee, Louis White, upstairs. Annie and Charles were on the customers' side of the Fitzroy for the first time when the morning regulars appeared, and after a while the Guv and his lady slipped away. The Fitzroy was under new management.

The money left over from the Pennies From Heaven fund was distributed to the many representatives from charities that had been present at the party. Roger Bannister, still the man of the moment after his record-breaking under-four-minute mile, had a cheque for £500 on behalf of the Duke of Edinburgh's charity – the National Playing Fields Association, and the Actors' Orphanage received £100, as did the Sunshine Homes For Blind Babies at Northwood and the National Spastics Society. Other organistions given money were the Residential School for Deaf Jewish Children - £75, the School for Deaf Children in Hereford via Gilbert Harding - £50, the Louis Glancy Home in Manchester, through Mrs Louis Golding - £25. The ceiling collection that night which was £568 18s 4d went to Save the Children Fund. In fact over the whole time at the Fitzroy in excess of £30,000 had been collected for charity, a splendid achievement. Charles and Annie announced that two trust funds would be set up as they wanted the generosity of the customers never to be forgotten. These were opened at the Midland Bank, Tottenham Court Road in the sum of £500 each. The trusts were to be called the Allchild Pennies From Heaven Trusts. The first one was for the 4th Surbiton Ajax Seas Scouts towards the maintenance of TS *Fitzroy* and the second was for an annual holiday for a needy child residing in the Borough of St Pancras irrespective of colour, race or creed to be selected by the Town Clerk and the Mayor of St Pancras. Both trusts still carry on today.

The Allchilds moved to a flat in Ridgemount Gardens, within Fitzrovia, where they were to live happily for the rest of their lives. Charles now hung the oil-painting of Pop in his office in the flat, along with his prized personal collection of water-colours by Nina, Rowley Smart and Geoffrey Nelson. Many friends popped in to see them and received as warm a welcome as ever in the Fitzroy. Sadly, the famous collection had to be sold eventually because of the problems of storage in the flat, and most went to the United States. It had all been carefully documented by Charles.

For their part Charles and Annie planned to go to America and look up Rosalie and the other members of the family there. Sally was to go with them though she was not so keen as she was madly in love with a rubber technologist called Arthur Fiber. She finally relented on condition that she could get engaged to Arthur. They left in autumn 1957 on the latest Stratocruiser. The first stop after New York was Chicago, where they boarded the famous train 'The Chicago Chief'. As they left the station and drove towards their hotel Annie yelled out and pointed at a huge hoarding. It proclaimed, *Kleinfeld Construction Company*. So they were able to trace the family and for the next three months they travelled to Los Angeles, San Francisco, New Orleans, Miami, Nassau and Jamaica. In Phoenix, Arizona, the Chief Federal Judge, Charles Berstein, turned out to be a distant relation. The final part of this fantastic adventure was the voyage home on the *Queen Mary*, but for Sally the highlight was the moment she saw Arthur running along the deck of the liner to greet her soon after it docked in Southampton.

Sally and Arthur were married on 23rd June 1957 at the Walm Lane Synagogue in Cricklewood. The reception was at the Dorchester. Guests included Ralph Reader, Jack and Babs Capstick, Bob and Billie Fabian and many other Fitzrovians, Wynford Vaughan-Thomas proposed the toast 'To the Hosts'. The great occasion was humorously described in Simon Ward's 'Inside Information' column in the *Daily Sketch* on Monday, 24th June 1957 under the heading 'Useful'.

> Useful to have the landlord of a famous pub in the family. Sally, dark-haired 21-year-old daughter of Charles Allchild, ex-owner of Soho's Fitzroy Tavern, was married yesterday at Cricklewood Synagogue to rubber technologist Arthur Fiber. Some of the old regulars from the Fitzroy were put to work at the Dorchester Hotel later. They got a professional TV commentator, Wynford Vaughan-Thomas, to make one of the speeches. Fabian of the Yard was handy if they needed anyone to keep an eye on the silver. Fred Narborough (the former detective) of the *$64,000 Question*

Programme was sitting in the corner drinking champagne – just in case one of the guests had a jackpot question to ask!

Over the next few years Charles and Annie enjoyed many cruises which took them to almost every part of the world, always meeting up with Fitzrovians. One such reunion was with Will Lawther on the P. & O. cruise ship, SS *Chusan*. Will was so pleased to see his old friends and he signed a photograph of Annie and himself *To Annie and Charlie, This brings memories of happy days at Britain's most famous pub 'the Fitzroy'. May that memory never fade, Just linger on. Will Lawther 20 Dec. 66.*

Annie and Charles were often featured in local newspapers. Articles about them, and the Fitzroy appeared in the *Vancouver Sun* in 1954, the *New Zealand Post* in 1955, the *Morocco Mail* in 1962 and the *Malta Times* in 1971 to name but a few.

After attending a special lunch organised by Age Concern of Greater London in October 1983 for those who had devoted their lives to helping others through charity, Annie and Charles were interviewed on *Thames News*.

'What have you got out of your years at the Fitzroy?' Annie was asked.

'Satisfaction and a lot of pleasure,' came the reply.

One final holiday was when they were approaching their eighties. Sally persuaded them to go on the *Orient Express* to Venice, where they could stay in the same hotel they had spent their honeymoon fifty years before, and to cap it all, fly back on Concorde. The flight on Concorde fulfilled Annie's greatest ambition, a great contrast to the days of looping the loop with Ross. Arthur and Sally were also invited as it was their pearl wedding year. But on their return home Charlie was awakened one night by a terrible banging in the flat. Someone was trying to break the door down. He called the police but by the time they arrived the would-be burglars had taken off. Though he saved the day, the frightening experience took its toll and he was never the same again. Soon Charlie became very ill and had to be admitted to University College Hospital, where on 18th July 1988 he passed away.

After eighty-five years of her life in Fitzrovia, Annie was at last persuaded that the time had come to leave Ridgemount Gardens and move to a retirement flat near Arthur and Sally in Northwood. Both Sally's children, Miriam and Jonathan, were adored and idolised by Annie. On 1st July 1989 Annie was invited back to open the festival which had now become a regular event within the Borough of Camden. Fitzrovia was now an official area within its boundaries. This was to be her final visit to her beloved patch of London, the one that she had given its name to, for Annie really was the 'Mother of Fitzrovia'.

Annie in turn died on 24th December 1989. She embodied the spirit of the Fitzroy and carried the flame for thirty-seven years at the Tavern. Welcoming, yet determined, a formidable businesswoman, but caring and benevolent, she was truly an amazing lady.

But perhaps the fitting testimonial to Annie and the Fitzroy came from James Norbury.

'To me, and I know I speak for thousands of others, the Fitzroy Tavern is much more than a London public house. It is part of the history of London, in fact it has become part of the fabric of our inheritance and... from personal experience is just as significant to visitors from all parts of the world as Buckingham Palace... In my own travels throughout Europe, I have been asked in Zurich, in Stockholm, in Copenhagen, in Venice, in Rome, in Milan, do I know the Fitzroy Tavern and is it as fabulous as the foreign correspondents have led them to believe when they have read about it in their newspapers? It is not only a pub [but] a landmark of the literary, artistic and social history of our times... Mrs Allchild has carried on the tradition her father laid as the foundation of the Fitzroy; the same spirit of generosity, the same spirit of good fellowship, these still prevail and are the essence of the life of this London tavern.'

Today the Fitzroy Tavern still proudly stands on the corner of Windmill Street and Charlotte Street in the hub and heart of Fitzrovia. The exterior remains the same, but the interior has been changed over the years. The present owners, Samuel Smith Breweries, have recently refurbished the bar, and adorning the walls are photographs and posters from its illustrious past given by Sally Fiber. Judah, Charlie and Annie now look down on the customers, and Tom Driberg's article 'No Moaning In This Bar' explains to the uninitiated how the Tavern gave its name to the surrounding district. In the cellar there is a small intimate Writers Bar and the old hand-cranked lift remains. The clientele of course has changed – executives visiting the Tavern in their snatched lunch-hour, young people clutching their blue Dillon's carriers, and a sprinkling of American tourists. In the evenings the place hums with gaiety and laughter, especially when on the first Thursday of the month the members of the Doctor Who Fan Club hold their meetings downstairs. A local historical society also gathers there every Monday.

The area too has altered. There are new office blocks, and the most famous landmark is the Telecom Tower, which dominates the skyline. Even the Scala Theatre, scene of the last Fitzroy party, is no more, replaced by the headquarters of Channel 4 TV. Certainly Fitzrovia is now richer than when near destitute Bohemian artists lived a hand-to-mouth existence and drank their last coppers in the Fitzroy and other nearby taverns. But all these pubs remain, as do the restaurants like L'Etoile, Bertorelli's and the White Tower. L'Etoile still presents old-fashioned excellence in its beautifully presented classic French cuisine. On the first floor where Nina once occupied rooms is a luxurious banqueting suite. Bertorelli's, though no longer in the ownership of the family, still offers reasonably priced Italian food, while The Eiffel Tower changed its name to the White Tower in 1943 and is now a fine Greek restaurant. From its splendid position it surveys the length of Charlotte Street, just as Cottrell & Co., the dental manufacturers, look down Windmill Street.

So the old mixes with the new in present-day Fitzrovia, which comprises ninety-three avenues, closes, corners, courts, gardens, markets, mews, places, roads, squares, streets, ways and yards. Three fashionable art galleries have opened up in Windmill Street – the Curwen, New Academy and Rebecca Hossack's – and across the road is the oldest violin shop in the country, Edward Withers Ltd. Bookshops include French's Theatre Bookshop, the Index Book Centre and Lamb's Legal and Medical

Bookshop. Pollocks Toy Museum in Scala Street is an Aladdin's cave of Victorian toys, while Simon Baker Casemakers in Gresse Street make Victorian quality luggage to order.

Besides the huge advertising concerns such as Saatchi & Saatchi, a host of small businesses have sprung up – craftspeople, picture-frame makers, printers, florists, travel agents, architects, accountants, lens manufacturers, hi-fi and computer shops, art suppliers and shops selling jewellery, fabrics, furnishings, home accessories, cards and gifts. But it is the restaurants that reflect best the cosmopolitan nature of Fitzrovia. Every taste is catered for, with Chinese, French, Greek, Indian, Italian, Japanese, Nepalese, Spanish and Turkish. Cafés, take-aways, sandwich bars, brasseries and wine bars complete the culinary picture. In the streets, shops and eating establishments the visitor can hear an amazing jabbering of foreign tongues.

But at the moment there is an exciting new wave of enthusiasm sweeping through Fitzrovia. This fresh spirit is embodied in the Fitzrovia Restaurateurs' and Traders' Association, which replaced the Fitzroy Circle in which Desio Vaiani had played such a leading part. Its dynamic chairman is another restaurateur, Stefano Fraquelli, of the Spaghetti House Group and owner of the Villa Carlotta, Charlotte Street. Their first problem to face was the new stringent parking policy of Camden Council with its rash of double yellow lines. This severely affected the custom of many restaurants in the area. After a petition and a research project had been submitted to the council, the restrictions were raised. Flushed with this initial success. Mr Fraquelli set up the 'Fitzrovia Today' project to give Fitzrovia a higher profile and identity. Quite simply they plan to 'put Fitzrovia on the map' by demanding that Fitzrovia as such be marked on all *A-Z* guide books and that the tube station be rechristened 'Goodge Street/Fitzrovia'. A street map and guide book has already been prepared and, who knows, the next step could be to issue passports to this village-like community! A Fitzrovia Neighbourhood Association organise an annual Fitzrovia Festival and prints the free *Fitzrovia News.* So although the high tide of Bohemianism may have passed, a brave new dawn beckons for this cosmopolitan district. Fitzrovia may yet obtain its independence from the competing claims of the Boroughs of Camden and Westminster.

What then is this new spirit in Fitzrovia? Perhaps the best answer to the question is to quote from the Introduction to the *Fitzrovia Today Map and Guide.*

Fitzrovia's civilised Georgian face belies its vitality and the happy culture mix who have found in Fitzrovia a place to create the diverse and welcoming enterprises you see today.

From family-run restaurants to haute cuisine, small design & crafts studios to the creative giants of the communications industry – all look upon Fitzrovia as their natural home.

At the end of busy days Fitzrovia mellows, its cosmopolitan café life spills onto the pavements. With the greatest number of quality restaurants of any corner of London you're bound to find one you'll soon want to call your own.

Take a walk through the hidden mews and alleys of Fitzrovia to find that elusive gift that typifies individuality – the hallmark of Fitzrovia today.

Amid the modern tourists who venture into this unique enclave returns the old Fitzrovian. Automatically, like a homing-pigeon, he heads for the Fitzroy. Finding a spare seat in the Tavern, he reverently sips his beer and looks round fondly at the photographs on the walls. With a few pints inside him, he imagines Nina tottering on her bar stool – 'I'll have a large gin, m'dear,' – Judah Kleinfeld nodding gravely and stroking his beard as Augustus John and Tommy Earp talk about 'Der Dybbuk', Betty May hitching up her skirt and on all fours lapping milk from a saucer to whoops of laughter or Albert Pierrepoint cracking jokes with his mate Bob Fabian. As more drinks go down, he gazes up at the ceiling and fancifully sees darts bulging with money, the 'Pennies From Heaven'. The children's parties, Carl, the police raid, Tambi – a kaleidoscope of past faces and events spin round in his head. Finally this nostalgic reverie is broken as the landlord shouts, 'Last orders!' It is not Annie or Charles Allchild behind the bar, but their spirit lives on in what was once 'The Rendezvous of the World', the creator, centre and lifeblood of Fitzrovia, the Fitzroy!

POST SCRIPT

Since The Autobiography of the Fitzroy Tavern was first published in September 1995 it has promoted much interest in the area of London known as FITZROVIA and the fascinating clientele that frequented The Fitzroy, the Fitzrovians.

Authors and researchers have contacted me for information and material. These include Dr Rhian Davis of the Peter Warlock Society, researching for a book on the life of the composer, Anne Wichard of London on the life of Betty May knows as the 'Tiger Woman'. Heather Stafford of USA sought information on her mother Ivy Crane Wilson. Ivy was the "Stars Correspondent" on the newspaper *Reveille*, and became the confidante to many Hollywood Stars. She was an ardent customer who introduced many famous Hollywood Stars to the Fitzroy. Her daughter traced me after her mother died, and was intrigued having found a gift inscribed *"From Annie & Charles Allchild & Fitzrovians through the world!"* I was present when my parents gave this box to her mother. Ivy became a true friend. We made a point of visiting her at her home in Hollywood during a trip to America.

Daniel Farson's book *Soho in the Fifties* featured one of his famed photos taken of my Dad smiling proudly behind the bar of the Fitzroy after the case. Daniel described his brave stand against the police and how he characteristically fought and won the case. When the *Fitzrovia News* in December 1988 reviewed his book their comment was, "how the picture shows the mettle of the man." My book also brought me together with Dylan Thomas's vivacious daughter Aeronwy, President of the Dylan Thomas Society of Great Britain. She was writing a book based on her father's memoirs; Clive my co-author and I encouraged her to complete the book. Sadly it was published three weeks after she died.

My intrigue to know more about my grandfather Pop led me to become the catalyst of a major four-year project to research and record the history of the Jews of London's West End I will always be grateful to the then curator of the London Jewish

Museum Rickie Burman and the many wonderful people who helped us achieve our aim. These included my cousin Judi Herman who wrote a most successful musical *How the West End Was Won*. This was based on the lives of the Jewish community of London's West End and the Fitzroy story. The findings of this project can be read in Dr Gerry Black's book *Living Up West*. Gerry now calls himself an honorary Fitzrovian and I was so proud that The Fitzroy Tavern through the charity played such a part of this story.

My darling Arthur passed away on Boxing Day of 2009. His family too played a major part of this story and I could not have achieved everything I have ever undertaken without his help. Arthur and I together with our son Jon continued as Trustees of the Allchild Pennies From Heaven Trust until 2003. Directly and indirectly we have been able to raise hundreds of pounds for charities as a result of the publication of '*The Fitzroy*'. In 2003 the investment period for the money ran out. After careful consideration we decided that the time had come to wind up the Trust and hand back the capital to the beneficiaries.

The Mayor of Camden's secretary suggested Fitzrovia Youth in Action be adopted as our charity. This is a youth organisation started up by the residents of Fitzrovia as a way of preventing anti-social behaviour and drugs. It established a very successful football team and encourages the young children to help the older members of the community too. It reminded me of the wonderful Boy's Jewish Youth Club that was established in Fitzroy Square back in the 20's. I remember my husband Arthur's cousin Frank telling us "if it hadn't been for the club he would certainly have got into so much trouble because there would have been nothing to do". I met André Schott the club's dynamic organiser when we all got together in the Fitzroy to mark the millennium; he was familiar with the ideals of the Pennies From Heaven charity. He was thrilled and straight away suggested that they could use the money for an outing for the children. I was delighted; it could not be a more appropriate use for the money, that's what my grandfather had used the money for 85 years ago!

I could not "just hand" over the money from the Trust. Within a week I arranged for this to take place in the Fitzroy. The

Fitzroy's Manager, Peter, was elated with the idea and we arranged for the ' hand over' to take place 4 p.m. on the 14th May 2005. The timing worked out well as the children from Fitzrovia Youth in Action were able to be present after school. I contacted Margaret, the Mayor's secretary who has been my contact over many years and asked if the Mayor could attend. I was excited to receive an email back to say she would certainly be there and Harriet. I was not sure who Harriet was but delighted that someone from Camden Council would attend. I also contacted the local press.

It's funny how things work out. On the Monday of that week I had been asked to be the guest speaker at the Harrow Friendship Club. After over 30 years as a speaker I am now in semi-retirement but I enjoy speaking and I was thrilled to be asked as I could tell them about the winding up of Pennies From Heaven Trust. After the talk an elderly lady came up to me. "I used to live in Fitzroy Street", she said. "I knew your mother Annie, and I used to go on the outings. Do you know I am 96!"

As I arrived at the Fitzroy on the 14th Peter the manager was there to greet us. "You must meet my friend Alice," he said as he introduced me, "she knew your mother and used to go on the outings." Amazing after all these years twice in this week I had met two ladies who had gone on the original outings!

Five minutes to four, no one else had arrived. I was rather disappointed, however all I was concerned about was that André should be there to receive the £1000 for Fitzrovia Youth in Action. Suddenly I looked up; two members of the press were there, photographers, André, with others connected with the club accompanied by the children and then the Mayor in her chain of office, yes 'Harriet' as she insisted I call her! Margaret and another member of their staff Bob who I had often spoken to accompanied her.

Handing over the cheque does not look much so I had made up a presentation certificate with a picture of the first outing which I presented to André. I also made one each for the Mayor and Peter to keep as a memento of the occasion. I was thrilled with the way it all worked out but totally amazed when from nowhere suddenly the Mayor presented me with the most fantastic flower arrangement with *'the very best wishes and most grateful thanks of Camden'*. This of course called for more photos. One I will treasure always was taken of Arthur and me in front of the 8 by 5ft life size photo of my Dad which is displayed in the Fitzroy - Charlie serving drinks behind the bar. He was there, so were Annie and Pop; how proud they would have been to see their dream end in such a way after 85 years.

The event was reported in the *West End News* with a colour picture on the front page of me and the children and an article with pictures also appeared in the *Camden New Journal*. The Ajax Sea Scouts held a special ceremony at which I presented them with their cheque for £1000. They are still a very vibrant group and remain one of 100 Sea Scout troops recognised by the Admiralty. In 2010 I proudly named another ex-naval ship Fitzroy. The troop has just established what Scouts call a 'Scout Active Support Unit' comprising a number of folks over the age of 18 who want to keep involved with the Group and to continue developing their own boating skills and at the same time 'put something back into Scouting'. The 'New Fitzroy' had a complete refit and is in regular use several times a week. I don't think there could be a better ending; however I still plan to support these and other charities through the publication of this new edition of my book.

But this is not the end! In 2013 a lady called Celine Hispiche put out a request for information about Betty May, the Tiger Woman, on Facebook. She was writing a musical based on her life, *Betty May Tiger Woman versus The Beast*.
www.BettyMayTheMusical.com

Betty was a former patron of the Fitzroy and friend of my parents who used to help at the children's outings. I contacted Celine and was most impressed with this very talented lady. The final scene is a celebration which takes place in The Fitzroy, with my Mum and Pop my grandfather, (view Chapter 7 Battle of the Fitzroy). I was delighted that I was able to help and see this production develop and look forward after its West End development shows for it to open at a London Theatre as soon as it is able. I was particularly thrilled when Celine and her partner Edwin Philpott asked if they could help start the Pennies From

Heaven Charity again to help London's children with me as its Patron. The new charity, *Fitzrovian Pennies*, is aimed at encouraging, supporting and enabling children of all ages to develop their talents through workshops, training and exhibitions in all fields of the arts. www.FitzrovianPennies.org

My book *The Fitzroy, The Autobiography of a London Tavern* has now earned its place in collectable first editions of Soho Books.

The Fitzroy Tavern in the 21st century is still the flagship pub of Fitzrovia, an "In Place" to visit in London, attracting a diverse clientele and much media interest. I extend sincere thanks to the current brewers Samuel Smith and its enthusiastic and dynamic Landlord Peter Deluliis. The Fitzroy's walls are again covered by a unique and fascinating display of photographs and documents depicting Fitzrovians past and present.

Augustus John's words are as apt today as when he uttered them in 1927,

"If you haven't visited The Fitzroy, you haven't visited London".

As a result of the upsurge of interest a number of new books have been published including:

FITZROVIA; London's Bohemia by *Michael Blackwell*, published by the *National Portrait Gallery, London* ISBN: 1 85514 256 2

Characters of Fitzrovia by *Mike Pentelow and Marsha Row*, published by *Felix Dennis* ISBN: 070 17349

Fear and Loathing in Fitzrovia by *Paul Willetts*, published by *Dewi Lewis* ISBN: 899235. Features the bizarre life of Julian Maclaren-Ross. The book includes photographs from my personal collection.

Soho in the Fifties by Daniel Farson, published by Michael Joseph Ltd (November 9, 1987) ISBN-10: 0718128761, ISBN-13; 978-0718128760

Living Up West, Jewish Life in London's West End by Dr Gerry Black, ISBN: 0 9511 61369

REVIEWS

Dr Marion Hardy, Physician
Your book was wonderful...so colourful and well written. The history was amazing. So often we visited the section of London you wrote about and had no idea of the lively history it held. We will definitely visit the Fitzroy on our next visit. It was a pleasure meeting you. Thanks for sharing your book with us. I hope our paths will cross again someday

Rosalind Joseph
I just wanted to let you know how much Gerald and I enjoyed your book. It was a story that had to be told. Thank you!

Aubrey Rose O.B.E. C.B.E. D.Univ.
What an excellent book it is! It is like a searchlight on a particular place and era, bringing back memories for some, illuminating the past for others.

.

VISIT FITZROVIA TODAY

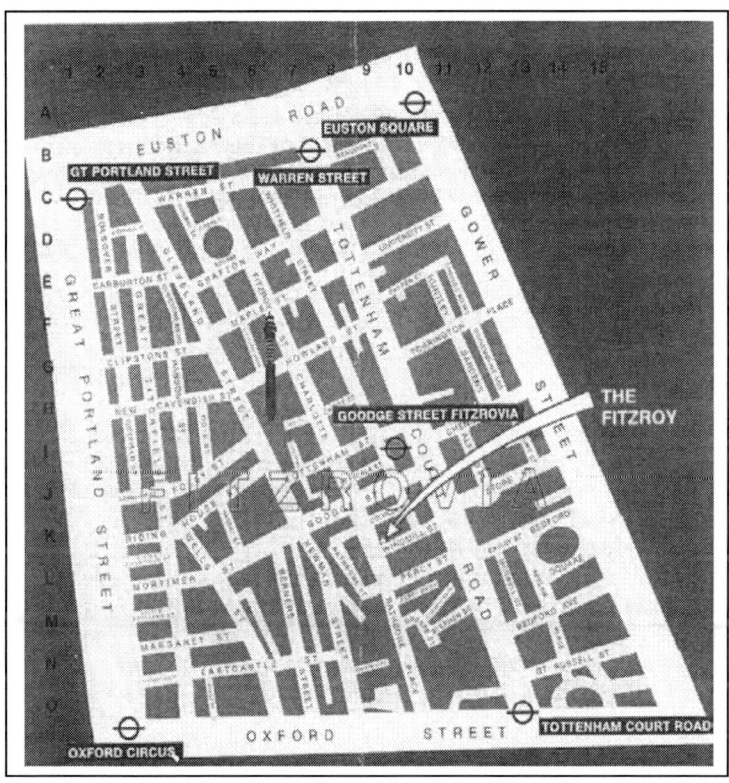

Reproduced by kind permission of *Fitzrovia Today*

Fitzrovia Street Index

ACKNOWLEDGEMENTS

We acknowledge and thank Denise Hooker and her publishers Constable for allowing us to use material from her biography, *Nina Hamnett, queen of bohemia* (1986), and in particular Julius Horwitz's conversation with her about war-torn London.

We are also indebted to Nick Bailey for historical references in his book, *Fitzrovia* (1981), and to Michael Parkin for quotations from Ruthven Todd's *Fitzrovia & The Road to the York Minster,* and to the publishers of *Albert Pierrepoint: Executioner* (1974) for the inclusion of extracts of this work.

Special thanks are due to John Arnold in Fairfield, Australia for information on Jack Lindsay.

Judi Herman's original musical Revue, *How The West End Was Won!,* which vividly portrays scenes from the Fitzroy and Kleinfeld saga based on material from the original transcripts of this book has added another dimension to the story.

The interest and support of Stefano Fraquelli, Chairman of 'The Fitzrovia Today' campaign, and the present management and staff of the Fitzroy is greatly appreciated.

We congratulate and extend our appreciation to Dennis Tuhrim for designing and drawing the book cover.

I would like to add my thanks to all at Book Printing UK for their friendly and professional help.

Further Acknowledgements re: New Edition

My appreciation again goes to; Aubrey Rose, Celine Hispiche, Edwin Philpott, Clive Powell-Williams, Judi and Steve Herman for proof reading, family and friends for their continued love and support.

BIBLIOGRAPHY

Bailey, Nick   *Fitzrovia*, Historical Publications,
                      London, 1981.
Farson, Daniel   *Soho in the Fifties,* Michael Joseph,
                      London 1987.
Hamnett, Nina   *Laughing Torso*, Constable, London,
                      1932.
Hooker, Denise   *Nina Hamnett, queen of bohemia*,
                      Constable, London, 1986.
Horwitz, Julius   *Can I get There by Candlelight*,
                      Atheneum, New York, 1984.
John, Augustus   *Finishing Touches*, Cape, London, 1964.
Lindsay, Philip   *I'd Live the Same Life Over*, Hutchinson,
                      London, 1941.
Maclaren-Ross, Julian *Memoirs of the forties*, Alan Ross,
                      London, 1965.
May, Betty   *Tiger Woman*, Duckworth, London, 1929.
Pierrepoint, Albert   *Executioner: Pierrepoint*, Harrap,
                      London, 1974.
Reader, Ralph   *It's Been Terrific*, Werner Laurie,
                      London, 1953.
Todd, Ruthven   *Fitzrovia & The Road to the York
                      Minster*, Parkin Gallery, London, 1973.

Other information collated from national and local newspapers, magazines, leaflets, brochures, personal letters, collection of photographs, paintings and drawings, Annie Allchild's autograph book, trial transcripts, visiting cards, recorded interviews and personal recollections.

INDEX